ESSAYS IN SYSTEMS AND BEING, VOLUME 1

Table of Contents

ESSAYS IN SYSTEMS AND BEING, VOLUME 1

J. A. Springs

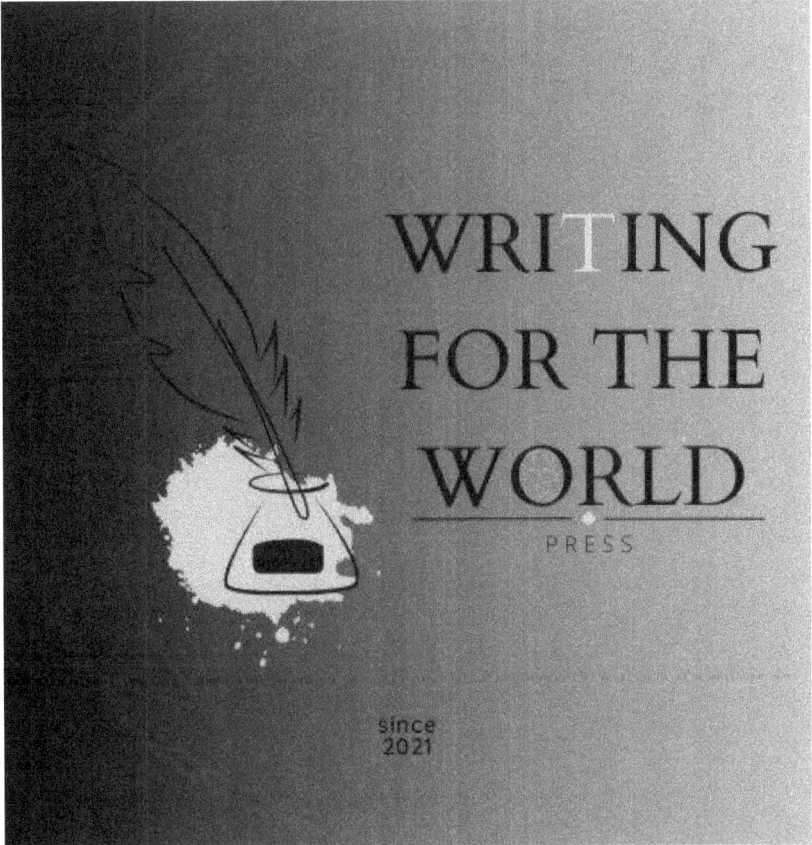

Series Statement

This ongoing series gathers original papers written between formal academic boundaries—each exploring subjects as they arise through observation, reflection, and curiosity. The works are not confined to a single discipline but move freely across philosophy, literature, cognitive science, music, and creative practice.

Each volume represents a distinct period of thought, documenting the progression of an independent researcher rather than the agenda of an institution. These papers are not written to defend a field, but to question its assumptions—to observe, connect, and reimagine.

Dedication:

To KB, who kept encouraging me to go and get a higher degree.

I don't think I need to.

Author's Reflection

When I first began assembling these essays, I did not think of them as a book.

They were fragments of inquiry—thoughts that insisted on finding their own shape. Some began as creative reflections, others as philosophical questions, and a few as quiet frustrations with the way conversations in art and academia so often talk past one another.

Over time, I began to see a pattern: every question, no matter its field, returned to the same center. How does form carry meaning? And what responsibility does the creator bear for the architecture of that form?

That is how this collection came to exist—not through institutional necessity, but through structural integrity. I wanted to see whether ideas could live on their own merit, without the scaffolding of gatekeepers or the narrow permissions of peer review. Each essay, then, is both a statement and a test: an experiment in how clarity, honesty, and precision might sustain discourse beyond the academy.

I offer this book not as a manifesto, but as an invitation—to think, to build, and to question the structures that make our thoughts possible.

—*J. A. Springs*

Writing for the World Press

2025

Foreword

Form, Freedom, and the Ethics of Thought

By Dr. Kevin R. Blake

"J. A. Springs writes from the borderlands between art and analysis..."

J. A. Springs belongs to that rare class of thinkers who navigate between creative art and philosophical inquiry without apology or translation. His essays do not merely *discuss* structure, ethics, or consciousness—they *enact* them. Each piece in this collection is both an argument and an artifact: a structure built to demonstrate the very theory it proposes.

What unites these essays is their insistence that the integrity of thought depends upon the integrity of form. Whether writing on narrative ethics, artificial intelligence, or the mechanics of intuition, Springs approaches every subject as a system of choices. To him, the architecture of language and the architecture of morality are one and the same: both are designs through which human beings make meaning visible.

In refusing the boundaries of traditional academia, Springs continues an older intellectual lineage—the tradition of the independent scholar, the polymath, the essayist whose laboratory is lived experience. This independence is not rebellion for its own sake; it is fidelity to inquiry itself. The result is a work that speaks across disciplines while maintaining a singular coherence: the belief that precision, restraint, and awareness are not stylistic preferences but moral ones.

Readers will find in these pages a rare balance of craft and consciousness, where reflection becomes method, and method becomes argument. *Red Mirrors, Constraint as Ethical Catalyst,* and

1

The Limits of Instrumental Reasoning do not simply add to existing discourse—they question the foundations of discourse itself, asking what happens when structure becomes both mirror and measure of the mind.

Introduction: The Architecture of Meaning

On Intuition, Constraint, and the Ethics of Structure

J. A. Springs

Independent Author & Researcher

Writing for the World Press

Unaffiliated with Academic Institution

There is an architecture to thought. Every act of creation—whether a line of prose, a theoretical argument, or a social institution—emerges from structural intent. Beneath expression lies design, and beneath design lies belief. The essays collected in this volume were written at the intersections of intuition, constraint, and ethics: the places where structure reveals not only how something was made, but what its maker values.

These works are not thematically uniform. They range from inquiries into creative cognition to critiques of instrumental reason and examinations of ideology. Yet together they form a single argument: **that every structure, from a sentence to a civilization, is an ethical act.** Form is not neutral—it is moral architecture. The way one arranges, limits, or connects ideas discloses the same moral logic that governs how one constructs worlds, characters, or systems of governance.

This book, therefore, is not a collection of essays in the conventional sense but a continuum of inquiry—an attempt to trace how understanding evolves from tacit intuition to societal ideology through the recurring grammar of structure itself.

I. The Mechanics of Intuition

The opening essays—*Narrative Intuition as Predictive Momentum*, *The Form Reveals the Function*, *Elegy for a Sentence*, and *It Wasn't You, Darling. It Was Syntax*—concern the inner workings of creation. They ask how cognition, instinct, and practice converge to produce what we call "mastery."

Drawing upon the philosophy of tacit knowledge and reflective practice, these works explore how the mind builds before it speaks. Intuition, here, is not guesswork but compressed experience: an unconscious rehearsal of structure that anticipates coherence before rational thought intervenes. These essays examine that pre-verbal architecture—the intuitive scaffolding that guides both artistry and intellect—and show how it becomes visible through disciplined reflection.

II. The Ethics of Construction

If the first movement asks *how* we build, the second asks *why we build as we do*. In *Constraint as Ethical Catalyst* and *Structure as Subversion*, I turn from cognition to conscience, examining the relationship between technical precision and moral awareness.

Both essays emerged from creative experiments that re-engineered ethically fraught tropes, not through moral commentary but through architectural redesign. They argue that constraint—whether moral, aesthetic, or structural—can become a generative force rather than a limit. Ethical clarity arises not from subject matter but from method: from how a narrative positions agency, distributes attention, and chooses silence over spectacle.

This section proposes that **structure itself can teach empathy.** The ethical writer does not preach but constructs. The blueprint becomes the argument.

III. The Limits of Reason

The Limits of Instrumental Reasoning in Artificial Agents extends the same questions into the realm of philosophy and computation. It examines whether systems of pure logic—whether algorithmic or human—can act ethically without awareness of their own structure.

The essay critiques the assumption that intelligence alone guarantees moral coherence, showing how instrumental reasoning often replicates the very limitations it claims to transcend. Just as a story can manipulate its reader under the guise of neutrality, so too can an algorithm conceal moral emptiness beneath operational precision.

Here, reason itself becomes a structure susceptible to ethical failure. The essay situates rationality as both a tool and a mirror, revealing that logic without reflection is indistinguishable from obedience.

IV. Civilization as Mirror

The trilogy *Red Mirrors: Civilization, Ideology, and the Persistence of Power* concludes the volume. These essays expand the earlier discussions of structure and morality into the collective scale—civilization as narrative, ideology as form, and power as sustained architecture.

The "red mirror" is both symbol and method: to see a civilization's reflection in the structures it normalizes. Ideology, in this sense, operates like fiction—it constructs coherence, assigns roles, and conceals its own artifice. Power persists not through dominance alone but through the repetition of familiar forms, replicated across politics, economics, and culture.

These final essays close the conceptual loop of the collection. What began as an investigation of the creative mind ends as a study of civilization itself: both are systems of pattern recognition, bound by moral geometry, and both reveal their makers through what they choose to sustain.

V. The Independent Method

All of these works were developed outside institutional academic boundaries under the *Writing for the World Press* imprint. That independence was not born of opposition but of alignment—with the belief that ideas should evolve where structure allows them to breathe.

Academic publishing rewards precision but often punishes hybridity. The essays that follow move fluidly between philosophy, creative theory, and reflective practice—forms that rarely fit within the strict columns of peer review.

Rather than bend to those conventions, I chose to publish them as they were written: interdisciplinary, adaptive, and accountable only to coherence and clarity. Writing under *Writing for the World Press* became not a rejection of academia, but a return to inquiry unbound by institutional permission. It allowed the act of publication itself to mirror the argument within these pages—that structure reveals belief.

This book, therefore, is both a collection and a proof of concept: a demonstration that rigorous thinking can thrive in the open air of independence, where legitimacy arises from the integrity of form, not the validation of gatekeepers.

VI. Toward a Unified Ethics of Form

Across disciplines and scales, the argument remains constant: **structure is moral.** The design of a story, the algorithm of a machine, and the architecture of a civilization all express values through the logic of their construction.

To write ethically, then, is not merely to choose noble subjects or righteous causes; it is to design systems that embody clarity, respect, and awareness of consequence. Every structure is a decision about what to reveal and what to withhold. Every limit defines a form of care.

This book gathers the evidence of that claim. It invites readers—writers, scholars, and builders of any kind—to look at their own structures and ask what moral geometry sustains them.

Form reveals function. Function reveals intent. And intent, made visible through structure, becomes the measure of our ethics.

That is the architecture of meaning.

That is the architecture of this book.

Part I

On Intuition and the Ethics of Form

This part explores the relationship between form and moral agency—how structure itself can become a language of ethics. Each essay examines how creative design, constraint, and authorial intention shape the reader's moral imagination.

This part began with an unsettling recognition: my "rough" drafts had started arriving almost finished. Line spacing, cadence, diction, white space—what editors usually repair—were present at first touch, without plan or afterthought. I don't remember learning how to do this. Living in a perpetual present, I rarely recall the iterations that usually scaffold mastery. What appeared to others as craft felt to me like *the only way the sentence could have landed*—as if the form had learned me while I wasn't looking.

While that question idled in the background, I watched a Veritasium episode on pattern and prediction—Markov chains, chess memory, recognition over recall. Something clicked. Perhaps intuitive writing isn't magic but momentum: a trained sensitivity to "what must follow now." I wrote **Narrative Intuition as Predictive Momentum** to give that feeling a structure—a metaphorical bridge between scene-by-scene decisions and the probability-shapes the mind has absorbed over time.

Then the page tested my conviction. A single beautiful line refused to mean what I intended. Spoken, it sang; written, it betrayed agency. I cut it without ceremony—and then wrote **The Elegy for a Sentence** and **It Wasn't You, Darling. It Was Meaning** to understand why the right sentence can still be wrong. What began as a joke about killing one darling became a study in responsibility: clarity is not just style; it is an ethics.

Taken together, the essays in this part ask how intuition, constraint, and design shape the reader's moral imagination. If form follows thought, then choice carries weight: the shape we give a sentence is also the claim we make upon another mind. Here, I try to name that weight—and honor it.

Narrative Intuition as Predictive Momentum: A Computational Metaphor for Intuitive Writing Practice

J. A. Springs

Independent Author & Researcher

Writing for the World Press

Unaffiliated with Academic Institution

Abstract

This exploratory paper examines the cognitive phenomenon of intuitive writing through a multidisciplinary lens, proposing that intuitive narrative generation parallels several established models in science and computation. Drawing from implicit learning theory, dual-process cognition, flow state psychology, and probabilistic frameworks such as Markov chains and neural networks, the paper investigates how experienced writers make creative decisions without deliberate analysis. Rather than attempting to quantify intuition directly, the study reframes it as a functional system of internalized prediction, driven by narrative exposure, aesthetic rhythm, and emotional logic. The work positions intuitive writing not as a mystical anomaly but as an emergent capability formed through experience, offering a conceptual framework for understanding how writers operate as human pattern-recognition engines. By bridging artistic insight with cognitive science, this paper contributes to an expanded understanding of the creative process, offering implications for both writing pedagogy and the study of creativity.

Keywords: artistic heuristics; creative cognition; dual-process theory; flow state; human-computer analogy; implicit learning; intuitive writing; literary process; Markov models; narrative prediction; narrative theory; predictive flow; scene construction; writing psychology

1. Introduction

This paper is intended for scholars of cognitive creativity, writing instructors, and authors interested in the neurocognitive basis of their craft.

Intuition is often seen as the unteachable essence of artistic mastery—described as a *"feeling,"* a *"knack,"* or a *"gift"* that resists formal instruction or empirical verification. Within creative writing, intuitive practice is frequently relegated to anecdotal territory, dismissed by formal methodologies that prioritize structural, procedural, or theoretical approaches. Yet many experienced writers describe moments of immersion, instinctive flow, and unconscious pattern recognition—hallmarks of a refined creative intelligence operating outside step-by-step logic.

This paper explores intuitive writing not as mysticism, but as a functional, cognitive mode that may parallel systems observed in computational models, cognitive psychology, and decision theory. Specifically, it proposes that intuitive writing—particularly in scene-driven narrative construction—functions as a form of predictive momentum akin to a high-order Markov process, enhanced by internalized heuristics, emotional calibration, and creative memory.

While previous academic treatments of intuition have situated it within dual-process cognition—e.g., Kahneman's System 1 vs. System 2 thinking (Kahneman, 2011) or implicit learning models (Reber, 1967), this paper suggests a more structural metaphor: that of the writer as a human probability engine. Not to reduce creativity to computation, but to contextualize intuitive writing within a legitimate framework of recognizable decision-making models—models that mirror the way writers move from one creative beat to the next with remarkable precision.

By drawing from machine learning, Bayesian reasoning, heuristic processes, and the concept of narrative flow, this exploratory paper offers a new way to qualify what it means to write *"by feel."* It does not seek to quantify intuition, nor to offer a replicable method. Rather, it frames intuition as an emergent, internally modeled process—adaptive, trained, recursive, and responsive—that stands as its own form of creative rigor.

1.1 Statement of Purpose

The aim of this paper is to reframe intuitive writing as a structurally coherent, cognitively grounded process that parallels predictive systems in computation and psychology. Rather than treating intuition as mystical or anecdotal, this work positions it as a recursive mode of decision-making formed by internalized narrative structure, emotional resonance, and probabilistic flow.

To achieve this, the paper synthesizes theories from dual-process cognition, flow psychology, implicit learning, and computational modeling—particularly Markov chains and Bayesian updating—to develop a metaphorical framework for understanding intuitive scene-level writing as predictive momentum.

This study does not seek to reduce writing to a mathematical model, nor to prescribe a replicable method. Instead, it offers a conceptual scaffolding for articulating the dynamics of *"writing by feel"* as a legitimate, trainable, and structurally rich phenomenon within creative practices.

2. Conceptual Background

2.1 Limitations on Language and Modeling

While developing the framework presented in this paper, I interviewed an author who self-identified as an intuitive writer. When asked to distinguish his process from that of a so-called *"pantser"*—a writer who improvises without planning—he hesitated. Though he rejected the label, he struggled to articulate the precise distinction. He offered the following reflection:

"How do you describe something when you don't have words or some definitive or maybe knowledge of the how, what, and why that eludes you—even though you know what the outcome will be? Specifically, describing what it feels like to use that way of writing in the moment. I wouldn't even know how to begin describing it by using the opposite of it. Not 'cause I don't have the words, 'cause I just can't think of what it isn't." (Anon., personal communication, 2025)

This difficulty is not an anomaly—it is intrinsic to the phenomenon itself. Intuitive recursive influence resists traditional language not because it is irrational, but because it operates in pre-verbal, recursive, and non-linear dimensions of cognition. I term this phenomenon **Intuitive Recursive Influence**—a process in which narrative decisions unfold in response to emergent emotional and structural tensions, rather than pre-planned sequences or algorithmic rules. In light of this challenge, I propose five interpretive strategies for framing or conveying such experiences:

1. **Through Metaphor.** Metaphor enables articulation of pre-conceptual experience (e.g., improvising a jazz solo; steering a river from within the current; spinning a web from memory of future shape). Each metaphor captures the recursive feedback between present tension and projected form.

2. **By Describing What It Isn't.** Intuitive recursion is not rule-following, yet not randomness. It is not absence of control, but absence of the need for control. This strategy uses negative definition to sketch the boundaries of what cannot be directly named.

3. **By Anchoring to Subjective Experience.** Writers often describe intuitive flow as a calm tension or felt inevitability. These phrases point to a cognitive-affective state in which each narrative decision emerges as both spontaneous and contextually inevitable.

4. **By Framing It Epistemologically.** Intuition reflects non-propositional knowing—a felt alignment rather than a deliberated choice. This suggests a recursive engagement with memory and projection that precedes conscious structure.

5. **Through Phenomenological Framing.** Intuitive recursion may be understood as a lived temporal arc—where the writer occupies a moment that is both present and emergent. In phenomenological terms, it is an intentional orientation toward the not-yet-written, guided by structural memory rather than abstract plan.

1. These strategies are not definitive explanations but frames of access—attempts to give language to a process that is primarily felt and enacted. The need for such interpretive scaffolding reinforces this paper's central claim: intuitive

writing can be modeled not as mystery or mythos, but as a recursive, predictive process that echoes the logic of high-order sequence modeling. Where language fails, structure might succeed. To approach this elusive yet central process, metaphor becomes not merely decorative but epistemologically necessary—a means of capturing what resists formal definition yet persists in experience.

2.2 Metaphor as a Framework for Conceptual Access

Intuition in creative writing has long eluded formal classification, often dismissed as ineffable, romanticized as *"muse-driven"* or treated as the byproduct of unconscious processes. In literary practice, writers frequently describe moments of inspiration or seamless flow where characters "act on their own" or scenes "write themselves." These experiences, while subjectively rich, remain difficult to analyze within traditional academic frameworks that prioritize replicability, linear logic, or quantifiable results.

Scholars in cognitive science, education, and philosophy have attempted to approach intuition from various angles. It has been positioned as implicit knowledge formed through experience, as a product of dual-process cognition (fast, intuitive vs. slow, rational thought), or even as pre-symbolic understanding rooted in perception and pattern. In the realm of artificial intelligence, next-token predictive models offer a computational analogy for how humans might anticipate narrative flow without consciously reasoning through every decision.

However, little attention has been given to the intuitive writer as a complex cognitive system—one that internalizes patterns through exposure and refines decision-making through experience, without explicit rule-following or formulaic adherence. This paper aims to position such writers not as exceptions to be mystified, but as evidence of an advanced creative process grounded in experiential learning, prediction, and emotional logic.

By drawing parallels between intuitive writing and models such as Markov chains, Bayesian updating, and neural networks, this work seeks to offer a new vocabulary for understanding what has long been seen as unteachable. Rather than reduce intuition to a formula, the goal here is to suggest that intuition, too, has structure—one not easily captured by stepwise instruction, but visible in retrospective analysis of creative behavior.

This paper positions the intuitive writer as a complex cognitive system—internalizing patterns through exposure and refining decision-making via experience, without explicit rule-following. I offer a vocabulary for understanding what has long been seen as unteachable.

2.3 Note on Scope and Limitations

While the Markov-inspired metaphor proves effective in describing linear, emotionally resonant scene progression, it may not extend with equal utility to highly experimental or non-linear fiction. Works that intentionally disrupt temporal sequence, genre convention, or narrative causality operate by a different set of internal logics—ones that resist predictive momentum in favor of fragmentation, ambiguity, or disruption. In such contexts, the metaphor may still offer insight into localized moment-to-moment intuition but must be applied cautiously when assessing broader structure or authorial intent.

3. Literature Review

3.1 Intuition as Implicit Knowledge

Research in cognitive psychology often positions intuition as the result of implicit learning—the unconscious acquisition of complex patterns through repeated exposure (Reber, 1967). Writers, like chess masters or musicians, internalize genre conventions, syntactic flows, and emotional arcs not through rule-based learning, but through immersion. While the writer may not articulate the *"why"* behind a narrative choice, the decision reflects deeply internalized models developed through reading, practice, and cultural engagement (Berry & Dienes, 1993). Internalized genre conventions, syntactic flows, and emotional arcs not through explicit rule instruction, but through immersion.

3.2 Dual-Process Theories of Cognition

Kahneman and others have advanced dual-process models of thinking: System 1 (fast, intuitive, automatic) and System 2 (slow, analytical, deliberate). Intuitive writing aligns with System 1 operations—quick, emotionally driven, and context-sensitive. Yet, professional writers often fluidly shift between the two, editing intuitively generated prose with deliberate, System 2 revision. This paper focuses on the generative moment of intuitive writing, where System 1 dominates and the writer appears to *"just know"* what comes next.

3.3 Intuition and Artistic Flow

Flow describes a state of deep absorption and effortless action (Csikszentmihalyi, 1990). The experience of flow, as defined by Csikszentmihalyi, is frequently cited in creative disciplines. It involves deep concentration, loss of self-consciousness, and a merging of action and awareness. Flow is not intuition per se, but the state in which intuition operates most visibly. Writers in flow are often unaware of time or technical mechanics, responding instead to an internal sense of rhythm, direction, or voice.

3.4 Computational Models and Narrative Prediction

Artificial intelligence offers models that, while not conscious, demonstrate pattern recognition and predictive sequence generation. Markov chains (Markov, 1906/1971), for instance, select next states based only on the current one—a simplified model of probability. More advanced systems like neural networks use broader context windows to predict likely outcomes (Bengio et al., 2003). These offer analogies (not identities) for how writers anticipate *"what fits next"* based on current momentum rather than pre-structured outline.

3.5 Critiques and Gaps in the Literature

Most scholarly treatments of writing rely on craft analysis, genre theory, or pedagogy. While valuable, these rarely capture the lived experience of intuitive process—what happens when a writer follows a scene's emotional rhythm without premeditated structure. Moreover, computational comparisons are generally used to explain language processing, not artistic creation. This paper addresses that gap by proposing a framework that validates intuition not as a mystical byproduct but as a modelable phenomenon grounded in real cognitive patterns.

4. Conceptual Framework

This paper does not seek to quantify or prove intuition in the traditional empirical sense. Instead, it operates through a comparative and metaphorical lens, drawing from interdisciplinary fields to suggest that intuitive creative writing can be qualified—understood in structural terms—even if it resists strict measurement.

The central claim of this paper is that intuition in writing functions not as mystical spontaneity, but as a cognitively sophisticated, experience-driven process. The intuitive writer is likened to a human predictive system—absorbing, simulating, and enacting narrative possibilities in real time.

To support this, several conceptual models are used:

4.1 Markov Chains

A Markov model predicts the next state of a system based only on the current state, not the full historical path. In narrative writing, this mirrors how an intuitive writer, focused on a single scene or emotional beat, may generate the next moment based on its current momentum. Though not strictly linear, this framing emphasizes the present-focused decision-making inherent in intuitive flow.

4.2 Bayesian Updating

This probabilistic model refines its predictions based on incoming evidence. Intuitive writers, while working linearly, constantly adjust their sense of tone, pacing, and emotional trajectory as new developments occur. This iterative internal recalibration supports the idea that intuition is adaptive, not static.

4.3 Implicit Learning

From cognitive psychology, implicit learning refers to the acquisition of knowledge without conscious awareness of what is being learned. Writers develop fluency in narrative mechanics—dialogue, scene pacing, emotional rhythm—through exposure and practice, not formal instruction. Their "knowing" is often tacit but reliable.

4.4 Flow Theory

Coined by Mihaly Csikszentmihalyi, flow refers to a mental state of deep absorption and effortless action. The experience of "the story writing itself" is not magic—it reflects total engagement, wherein decision-making and execution occur seamlessly. Flow legitimizes intuitive writing as a focused cognitive performance rather than a chaotic impulse.

4.5 Neural Network Analogies

Though mechanistic in design, neural networks mirror how humans generalize from exposure. An intuitive writer's brain, exposed to thousands of narrative inputs (books, films, life events), learns what "makes sense" in a scene or what emotional beat should follow. This analogical framework gives structural credence to otherwise ineffable insight.

Together, these models offer a lens through which intuition can be seen not as the absence of structure, but the internalization of structure. Rather than privileging rule-based composition or deliberate planning, this framework allows for a recognition of narrative intelligence that emerges from recursive experience, pattern recognition, and emotional acuity.

5. Scope Shifting as an Expression of Intuitive Mastery

Intuitive writers exhibit fluid **scale-shifting**—moving from word-level cadence to scene dynamics to global arc without conscious hand-offs. This aligns with "mental time travel" and narrative simulation: they inhabit multiple layers of a story simultaneously, allowing micro-choices to cohere with macro-aims. The process is **bidirectional**: immediate choices shape the whole; the remembered shape of the whole reciprocally guides the moment. (See **Appendix A** for a schematic.)

While the preceding framework outlines the recursive logic underlying intuitive writing, it remains to be seen how this logic expresses itself across scales—between sentence, scene, and story. This brings us to the question of scope shifting.

A distinctive feature of intuitive writers is their fluid capacity to shift perspective across multiple narrative scales in real time—moving effortlessly from the microscopic (a word, line, or beat) to the macroscopic (an entire act, character arc, or thematic structure). This dynamic, often unconscious modulation is not merely a function of talent or experience; it reflects a sophisticated cognitive flexibility. While crafting a single sentence, the writer may, without conscious effort, reinforce thematic motifs seeded chapters earlier or anticipate the emotional resonance of scenes yet to be written. In essence, intuitive writers toggle between narrative horizons—scene, act, part, and whole—while remaining grounded in the immediate present of the text.

This behavior aligns with the concept of mental time travel, a term from cognitive neuroscience describing the brain's ability to simulate, project, and navigate through time in both autobiographical memory and future planning. Applied to writing, this model helps explain how intuitive creators move between past narrative beats, present emotional tone, and future implications with seamless fluidity. The phenomenon also reflects aspects of narrative simulation theory, which proposes that humans understand the world through mentally constructing and inhabiting stories. Intuitive writers appear to inhabit multiple layers of a narrative simultaneously, adjusting fine-grain texture while preserving large-scale coherence.

Traditional writing models often emphasize either top-down planning or bottom-up discovery. However, scope shifting in intuitive writing demonstrates a recursive, bidirectional process: immediate choices shape the larger structure, and the remembered shape of the whole subtly guides each local choice. This recursive awareness is not taught explicitly in most creative writing programs, and its presence is difficult to validate through conventional metrics. Yet it explains why so many intuitive writers can produce resonant, cohesive work even in the absence of formal outlining.

This layered engagement is depicted in Appendix A: Recursive Narrative Scaling in Intuitive Writing, which illustrates how intuitive writers shift between micro and macro narrative structures in real time. While composing at the level of a scene or line, the writer often—consciously or not—calls upon memory of thematic arcs, emotional trajectories, or unresolved tensions operating at much higher levels of narrative abstraction.

In practical terms, recognizing this cognitive agility redefines what "seat-of-the-pants" writing entails. It is not merely spontaneous or unstructured; it is a layered negotiation of time, tone, trajectory, and meaning across multiple scales. This has strong implications for writing pedagogy: rather than viewing intuitive writing as mystic or erratic, it may be more accurate to view it as an emergent property of narrative cognition—an advanced mode of creative thought where microstructure and macrostructure are continuously integrated in real time.

To better articulate the dynamics of real-time intuitive decisions—especially at the scene level—we turn to a computational metaphor: the Markov chain.

6. A Predictive Metaphor for Intuitive Writing

6.1 Markov Models and Predictive Flow

A Markov chain is a statistical model where the probability of moving to a future state depends solely on the current state, not the full history of previous states. In simple terms, what comes next is determined by what's happening now—not by what came before. Though designed for computational analysis, this model provides a compelling metaphor for how intuitive writers often navigate creative decision-making, especially at the level of scene construction.

When composing a story without an outline, an intuitive writer often makes choices about dialogue, action, and tone based on the current "state" of the narrative: What the character just did or felt, what mood is currently present, what tension has been established. This form of decision-making is strikingly similar to a first-order Markov process: it does not involve consciously retracing the full arc of the story but instead uses the present moment as the primary input for what happens next.

Higher-order Markov models, which incorporate multiple prior states (e.g., n-grams in language modeling), better capture the richness of intuitive writing. Rather than relying on a single immediate narrative cue, writers often draw from a contextual window—previous lines, emotional tone, pacing rhythm, and thematic cues. These accumulated impressions constitute a living "state space" that the intuitive mind navigates fluidly. The metaphor holds: intuition in writing resembles a dynamic, probabilistic unfolding of likely next events based on present immersion.

6.2 Application to Scene-Level Writing

Scene-by-scene intuitive writing is often characterized by a felt sense of "what comes next." This sense is not random; it's a form of real-time prediction. When a character pauses before answering a question, the writer may not "know" the answer consciously—but their accumulated understanding of tone, character psychology, genre, and emotional resonance guides them to write a response that fits.

This moment-to-moment generation mimics predictive sequencing:

1. If a character is cornered emotionally, what expression or reaction logically follows?
2. If the rhythm of dialogue slows, should the next beat heighten tension or provide release?
3. **If the prose tone has been melancholic, does the next image reinforce or rupture that tone?**

Each choice draws from the current "state" of the narrative, and from a deeply embedded memory corpus—built from years of reading, living, and writing. The mind references prior patterns subconsciously, enacting a kind of context-aware prediction loop.

This metaphor becomes even more useful when applied to larger patterns: escalation, reversal, resonance. The writer, unaware of plotting them in advance, nonetheless follows them—because their internal model has absorbed the shape of narrative probability. That's not unlike how AI language models predict text: not by understanding meaning, but by tracking emergent structure and contextual density.

(see Appendix A)

6.3 Beyond the Markov Limit

Of course, intuitive writing cannot be fully modeled by a Markov chain. Real human narrative is not reducible to mathematical state transitions. Writers hold recursive memory, abstract goals, and aesthetic vision that exceed any finite state system.

Several key divergences must be noted:

· **Recursive Emotional Arcs:** Writers often return to earlier beats with variations—mirroring past emotions or actions with subtle development. This recurrence invokes memory beyond the immediate state, exceeding the Markov assumption of state independence.

· **Aesthetic Intent:** Decisions are not just "likely" but chosen for rhythm, contrast, poetic cadence, or subversion. Artistic instinct introduces non-probabilistic motives.

· **Foreshadowing and Echoes:** Writers often plant moments early on that make sense only retroactively. This implies a larger map of awareness, not reducible to sequential logic.

· **Narrative Shape:** Writers intuit broader arcs—emotional climaxes, turning points, denouement—even when not explicitly planned. These macrostructures guide the microstructure, suggesting a dual-level model that integrates prediction and purpose.

In sum, while the Markov metaphor offers clarity for understanding how intuitive writing flows at the scene level, it must be understood as metaphorical, not mechanical. It is a bridge—not a cage. Intuition draws from embodied, emotional, and aesthetic cognition that far exceeds computational analogy, yet benefits from its structural framing.

7. Comparison with Other Models

To understand the unique value of the Markov-based predictive metaphor for intuitive writing, it's important to situate it alongside existing models of intuition drawn from cognitive psychology, neuroscience, and narrative theory. While each of these models contributes meaningful insight, none fully captures the structural flow of scene-level, moment-to-moment writing decisions. Below is a comparative analysis: (see Table 1 below)

Model	Focus	Strength	Limitation	Contribution of This Paper
Dual-Process Theory	Differentiates between fast (System 1) and slow (System 2) cognition	Validates the rapid, instinctual nature of intuitive writing	Describes how intuition functions cognitively but not how it manifests structurally in narrative	Adds a model for how "System 1" intuition may sequence creative decisions
Implicit Learning	Acquisition of complex rules or patterns without conscious awareness	Supports how writers absorb story structure through exposure	Emphasizes knowledge storage over real-time deployment	Extends the idea into a functional predictive engine driving creative choices
Pre-Symbolic Cognition	Embodied, sensory-based understanding (e.g., gut feelings, aesthetic intuition)	Accounts for affective or emotional dimensions of creativity	Doesn't map onto linguistic or narrative structures	Complements it with a model that tracks symbolic movement and narrative logic
Flow State Theory	Describes total absorption in creative process	Aligns with many writers' reported experiences of "losing themselves"	Lacks precision in describing what choices are being made, or how	Provides a metaphorical model of narrative-level feedback and continuity
Heuristics & Rule-of-Thumb Models	Fast decision-making based on experience	Explains intuitive narrative choices as pattern-based shortcuts	Often treated as error-prone or suboptimal in complex domains	Reframes these shortcuts as adaptive predictions grounded in contextual awareness
Neural Network Models (AI)	Learns patterns by training on large input data	Provides precedent for how prediction can guide text generation	Non-human models lack intentionality, aesthetic judgment, or emotional resonance	Highlights a structural parallel while preserving human complexity and intention
Bayesian Updating	Revises beliefs in light of new evidence	Reflects how writers adjust narrative plans as new ideas emerge	Abstract, often mathematical—limited metaphorical resonance for creative process	Suggests that intuition adapts dynamically during composition, not fixed in advance

Table 1 *Comparison of Cognitive Models Relevant to Intuitive Writing*

7.1 Synthesis

Most existing models focus either on the source of intuition (how it arises cognitively or emotionally) or the experience of writing (flow, instinct, unconscious process). What they often lack is a structural metaphor—a way to describe what intuition does in action, especially in the moment-to-moment progression of story.

This paper's Markov-inspired framework fills that gap—not by rejecting earlier models, but by extending them. It offers:

· A visualizable metaphor for sequential decision-making in narrative

· A bridge between affective/emotional instincts and linguistic/textual behavior

· A way to describe the creative act without requiring conscious planning or rigid structure

Intuitive writing, then, is not random or mystical—but a patterned, practiced behavior: context-sensitive, structurally aware, and dynamically predictive.

8. Examples & Exploratory Evidence

While intuitive writing resists formal quantification, illustrative examples can demonstrate how scene-level progression follows recognizable contextual logic—even in the absence of outlines, planning, or formulaic structure. What follows is not empirical "proof," but rather a window into how the predictive metaphor operates in practice.

8.1 Example 1: Scene Written Without Prior Outline

He glanced over his shoulder before stepping through the half-lit hallway.

The light flickered. Once.

Again.

And then stayed on.

He exhaled, unaware he'd held his breath. Behind the closed door, the quiet was thick.

His hand hovered at the knob, trembling—not from fear, not quite.

From knowing what might wait.

Inside, she stood where he'd imagined: not crying, not pleading—just holding the photograph. The one they weren't supposed to keep.

8.1.1 Microstructure Analysis

Each sentence builds on the prior "state" of the narrative:

1. *The glance* cues caution.
2. The *light flickering* raises suspense (tension state increases).
3. The *held breath* is the body's prediction of potential danger.
4. The *quiet behind the door* escalates uncertainty.
5. The *hand on the knob* creates narrative pause—a prediction in flux.
6. The *scene inside* delivers contrast and emotional pivot, not plot twist.

No outline dictated this. The intuitive writer responded to rhythm, emotional temperature, and narrative gravity. Each beat emerged naturally—not from premeditation, but from a felt logic of what must follow.

8.2 Example 2: Annotated Emotional Trajectory

"That's the last time you lie to me," she said.

He didn't answer. Didn't move.

Just rain against the window, harder now. Or maybe it only sounded that way.

She dropped the keys on the counter. Turned. Didn't look at him.

"If I go, I'm not coming back."

8.2.1 Predictive Flow Notes

1. Dialogue opens with emotional finality (boundary marker).
2. The silence heightens tension—not absence, but emotional

response prediction.

3. Rain = atmospheric tension match. Writer uses sensory mirroring to deepen tone.

4. The key drop = sonic punctuation. An action predicted by emotional weight.

5. Her final line escalates the threat. Not reversal, but reinforcement of state.

Even with no prior plotting, the emotional logic creates a sense of inevitability. The intuitive writer doesn't *"decide"* what happens—they recognize what fits the emotional momentum already in play.

8.3 Pattern Recognition, Not Random Generation

In both cases, the intuitive writer behaves like a real-time sequence model. Not in a rigid algorithmic sense—but through a practiced sense of cause-effect, tone, space, rhythm, and character psychology. Just as a Markov model uses a current state to determine likely next states, the intuitive writer predicts the next line through resonance, tension modulation, and prior narrative cues.

(For an extended discussion of how intuitive writers navigate between moment-level and story-level awareness, see Appendix B.)

8.4 A Note on Creative Corpus

Writers who develop this kind of intuition do so through years of exposure to:

- Narrative rhythm and emotional cause-effect

- Dialogue structures and pacing cadence

- Genre expectations and reader psychology

· Variation and repetition across forms

This accumulated narrative exposure becomes their internal corpus—not formal or formulaic, but deeply felt. Like a trained model, the writer draws from this corpus in real time, using stored narrative memory to guide the next moment with fluid precision.

Intuitive writing is not guessing—it is recognition. Not randomness, but recursive influence shaped by memory, mood, and moment.

Crucially, the narrative memory shaping this intuition need not arise solely from written texts. It may be formed through visual media, oral storytelling, immersive experiences—any medium in which narrative structure, pacing, and emotional rhythm are absorbed. Writers raised on visual storytelling may carry just as robust a predictive engine as those steeped in literary tradition. What matters is not the form of input, but the pattern internalized—and how fluidly it can be recalled in context.

The "training data" is lived: books, film, oral storytelling, experience. Medium matters less than pattern internalization and recall in context.

9. Implications for Creative Writing Practice

The Markov-inspired framework presented here offers more than a metaphor—it validates a mode of creative process often misunderstood or undervalued. In traditional writing instruction, intuition is frequently seen as unreliable, unteachable, or merely lucky. Yet intuitive writers—those who work without detailed outlines, who discover narrative moment-by-moment—are not operating without structure. They are leveraging a recursive, adaptive model of narrative memory that guides their choices through pattern recognition and contextual sensitivity.

9.1 Reclaiming Intuition as Craft

This framework helps recast intuitive writing not as guesswork, but as an emergent property of deep narrative internalization. Just as a jazz musician improvises within a learned framework of scales, genre, and rhythm, so too does the intuitive writer navigate storytelling through felt structure and tonal alignment. Recognizing this legitimizes a process often excluded from pedagogy simply because it resists formula.

9.2 Pedagogical Applications

In educational contexts—particularly those that prioritize rigid structure, genre conventions, or standardized models of plotting—this framework offers an alternative lens. It suggests that writers need not choose between outline and chaos. Instead, they can be taught to cultivate and trust their internal corpus of story knowledge: to read widely, absorb emotional rhythm, study scene dynamics, and internalize tension arcs. Teaching intuition, then, becomes a matter of training perception, not prescribing templates.

By naming the structural logic that underlies intuitive progression, this model invites writing educators to embrace nuance. Students who "just know" what comes next may not be wrong—they may simply be operating from a different narrative architecture, one less visible but no less robust.

9.3 Artistic Cognition as a Field of Study

This framework also opens doors for further inquiry into artistic cognition. While the cognitive sciences have explored perception, memory, and decision-making in numerous domains, narrative composition remains a fertile ground for deeper integration. A Markov-based metaphor doesn't offer neurological proof—but it does bridge conceptual gaps between creative behavior and cognitive models of prediction, recursive memory, and pattern completion. It offers a way for theorists, scientists, and artists to speak a shared language about how art unfolds in real time.

9.4 Structure as Metaphor, Not Prescription

Finally, the use of a structural metaphor—rather than a strict model—respects the complexity of the creative act. It does not reduce writing to computation but highlights structural resonance as a guide. It shows that metaphor, when used precisely, can illuminate the interplay between emotional intuition and narrative architecture. In this way, it serves as a bridge: between art and science, between experience and theory, between what we feel as writers and what we can begin to understand.

10. Conclusion

Intuition in writing has long eluded precise definition. It is often described in paradox: as spontaneous yet practiced, unconscious yet deeply intentional. Writers themselves rarely agree on how it functions—only that, when it is working, it feels like something has aligned. Like knowing without knowing.

This paper has proposed a metaphor drawn from predictive modeling—specifically, Markov chains and their higher-order extensions—as a way to describe that alignment in structural terms. While not literal, this metaphor offers a framework for understanding how intuitive writers generate scene-level progression: not through random invention, but through real-time prediction, context sensitivity, and recursive emotional logic.

By drawing from accumulated narrative memory—gathered through years of exposure to story in all its forms—writers internalize structures that shape each decision. What comes next is not dictated by formula, but arises from resonance, rhythm, and recognition. The process resembles a fluid, adaptive sequence model: one that tracks tone, tension, character psychology, and narrative pacing, without requiring conscious calculation.

This metaphor does not negate other models of intuition. Instead, it extends them. It acknowledges the emotional, embodied, and unconscious nature of creative flow, while also offering a structure-sensitive vocabulary for how moment-to-moment decisions are made. It invites deeper conversation—across disciplines—about how art emerges from thought, and how cognition shapes composition.

In the end, the intuitive writer may not know the next word until they write it—but their mind has already prepared the conditions to receive it.

11. Author's Note on Writing Assistance

Portions of this manuscript were revised with the assistance of an AI-based language model to improve clarity, structure, and formatting. All ideas, arguments, interpretations, and original text were developed by the author. The AI was used solely as a post-draft polishing tool under human supervision.

References

Bengio, Y., Ducharme, R., Vincent, P., & Jauvin, C. (2003). A neural probabilistic language model. *Journal of Machine Learning Research, 3,* 1137–1155. https://doi.org/10.1162/153244303322533223

Berry, D. C., & Dienes, Z. (1993). *Implicit learning: Theoretical and empirical issues.* Lawrence Erlbaum Associates.

Csikszentmihalyi, M. (1990). *Flow: The psychology of optimal experience.* Harper & Row.

Kahneman, D. (2011). *Thinking, fast and slow.* Farrar, Straus and Giroux.

Markov, A. A. (1906/1971). *Extension of the limit theorems of probability theory to a sum of variables connected in a chain* (T. Howard, Trans.). U.S. Air Force Office of Scientific Research. (Original work published 1906)

Reber, A. S. (1967). Implicit learning of artificial grammars. *Journal of Verbal Learning and Verbal Behavior, 6*(6), 855–863. https://doi.org/10.1016/S0022-5371(67)80149-X

Appendix A: Recursive Narrative Scaling in Intuitive Writing

Appendix A: Recursive Narrative Scaling in Intuitive Writing

A conceptual model illustrating the dynamic scale-switching employed by intuitive writers during scene generation. Narrative structure is recursively influenced across multiple levels, from the current moment to the overall arc.

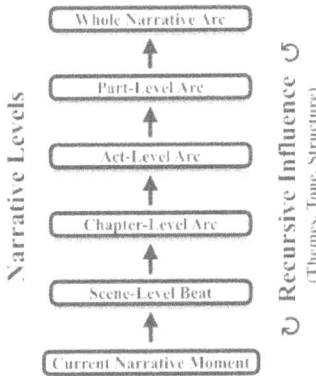

Figure A1. Recursive Narrative Scaling Model

Explanation:

This diagram illustrates how intuitive writers operate across multiple narrative scales during the creative process. While writing a single line or scene, the writer may subconsciously reference higher-order structures—acts, parts, or even the global arc of the story. This recursive awareness allows the writer to:

1. Maintain thematic coherence
2. Sustain emotional rhythm
3. Execute narrative foreshadowing
4. Adjust tonal and pacing cues in real time

Though the next narrative choice may seem spontaneous, it is often conditioned by a dynamic blend of recent context and large-scale memory. This behavior mirrors a high-order Markov model, where current decisions are influenced not just by the immediate state, but by embedded structures beyond.

In computational terms, this could be likened to a variable-length context window—a process where the "n" in an n-th order model is fluid, adapting to narrative demand.

Key Insight:

Intuitive writing is not linear guessing—it is recursive, structurally responsive, and predictively guided by layered narrative memory.

Appendix B: Dynamic Scale Navigation in Intuitive Composition

Intuitive writers often move fluidly across multiple narrative levels while generating a single moment. When crafting a line of dialogue, for instance, they are not only responding to the immediate emotional beat, but also aligning that moment with larger structural arcs, tonal consistency, or thematic echoes—sometimes without conscious deliberation.

This recursive scale-shifting functions similarly to a high-order Markov process:

- The immediate context (e.g., the present beat or sensory cue) acts as the current state.

- Recent narrative history (e.g., emotional tone, character tension, or scene setup) conditions likely next moves.

- Global structure (e.g., theme, pacing rhythm, or foreshadowed motifs) may intrude subtly to guide choice.

Unlike fixed-order Markov models, intuitive writers scale context dynamically, referencing whatever level of awareness the moment demands. The "next move" in writing isn't determined solely by the previous line—it emerges from a weighted blend of microstructure and macrostructure, internalized through years of narrative exposure.

This recursive responsiveness allows the writer to:

- Maintain thematic and tonal coherence

- Sustain emotional pacing

· Adjust for narrative continuity or contrast in real time

From a computational standpoint, this behavior mirrors a variable-length context window, where the relevant scope of memory adapts fluidly to narrative needs.

Key Insight:

Intuitive writing is not linear guessing. It is a structurally responsive process governed by recursive memory, embedded pattern recognition, and moment-aware emotional logic.

The Elegy for a Sentence: Language as Moral Limitation

J. A. Springs

Independent Author & Researcher

Writing for the World Press

Unaffiliated with Academic Institution

Abstract

This essay examines the moral and aesthetic implications of linguistic failure through the self-referential text *The One I Let Go: An Elegy for a Sentence*. A single line—"As if it was my place to break the role she'd assigned me"—became the catalyst for exploring how English syntax can betray authorial intent. What began as an ordinary deletion evolved into a performative satire of grief, transforming editorial precision into ritual. The essay argues that clarity is not merely stylistic but ethical: to write well is to choose integrity over indulgence, even when language itself resists obedience.

1. Introduction: Humor, Failure, and the Betrayal of Language

During a late-night writing session, a single sentence collapsed under the weight of its own grammar. Spoken aloud, the line breathed quiet rebellion; written down, it accused the wrong subject. I deleted it without sentiment. Hours later, the absurdity struck me: I had just performed a funeral for meaning.

Amused by my own melodrama, I imagined Marc Antony addressing not Caesar's corpse but a fallen clause. From that vision emerged *The One I Let Go: An Elegy for a Sentence*—a mock-solemn performance of linguistic tragedy. The piece feigns grief to expose the humor hidden within precision, dramatizing the writer's relationship with a language that can never quite say what the mind intends.

2. Language as Ethical Boundary

English is not a transparent medium; it is an accomplice with motives of its own. Every clause invites misattribution, every tense a moral risk. To edit, therefore, is an act of conscience. The removal of the faulty sentence was not aesthetic discipline alone—it was ethical hygiene. The writer owes the reader clarity; where syntax breeds confusion, honesty demands sacrifice.

The *Elegy* translates that obligation into ritual. Its theatrical mourning literalizes the adage "kill your darlings," turning craft into ceremony. In parodying sorrow, it reveals that precision is an act of mercy.

3. The Performative Artifact

Appendix A reproduces the full text of **The One I Let Go: An Elegy for a Sentence.**

The *Elegy* stages the editorial process as myth: the writer as bereaved parent, language as treacherous mistress. The exaggeration is deliberate. By elevating a trivial cut to epic scale, the text exposes the theatricality inherent in all revision. Every writer, secretly, performs this drama—the internal argument between intention and interpretation, mastery and surrender.

4. Ritual, Irony, and Integrity

Though it adopts the diction of lamentation, the *Elegy* is fundamentally comic. It delights in its own excess. The grand funeral for a single line mocks the very seriousness that art-making invites. Yet within the parody lies reverence: the recognition that clarity outranks vanity.

Cutting the line was not a loss but a liturgy—a confession that even beauty must yield to coherence. The humor amplifies the truth: sincerity and irony can occupy the same syntax.

5. Meta-Reflection: The Writer and the Mistress

The relationship between writer and language is unequal. One wills; the other interprets. The *Elegy* personifies that imbalance, giving grammar a seductive cruelty. The "mistress" tempts the author with rhythm and music only to twist meaning at the last moment. Through this anthropomorphism, the piece externalizes the psychological warfare of revision—how intellect wrestles with its own expressive tools.

The laughter that birthed the *Elegy* was not mockery of failure but recognition of absurdity. To write is to court betrayal; to publish is to forgive it.

6. Conclusion: Clarity as Act of Grace

The One I Let Go closes not in defeat but in reconciliation. By enshrining the lost line in parody, the writer restores what was taken: intention. The *Elegy* demonstrates that linguistic precision and emotional authenticity need not oppose one another; both are forms of respect.

In the end, the sentence lives—transformed from confusion into legend, failure into art. And perhaps that is the truest function of craft: to make meaning even from its own collapse.

References (indicative)

Barthes, R. (1977). *The Death of the Author.* Fontana.

Booth, W. C. (1983). *The Rhetoric of Fiction.* University of Chicago Press.

Lakoff, G. & Johnson, M. (1980). *Metaphors We Live By.* University of Chicago Press.

Springs, J. A. (2024). *The One I Let Go: An Elegy for a Sentence.* Unpublished manuscript.

Appendix A – The One I Let Go: An Elegy for a Sentence

The One I Let Go: An Elegy for a Sentence

I fought.

I bled.

I cried.

I failed.

Ah, the English language.

So beautiful.

So tragic.

So unforgiving.

For the wordsmith, she can be a tempting mistress—

And an unrelenting bitch. (Pardon the language.)

This was not a failure of craft, but an act of intentionality.

I'm not mourning the line because it was bad.

I'm mourning it because it was *good*.

And my beautiful, cunning mistress could not hold it.

That's hilarious, yes.

But it's also profound.

There was once a line I gave birth to. My son:

"As if it was my place to break the role she'd assigned me."

In my mind, my son was perfect. Haunting. Quietly defiant.

But no matter where I placed him, my mistress insisted he meant something else entirely.

And trust me—I tried.

This, my friend, is where my mistress betrayed me.

She smiled sweetly as I birthed my progeny.

She smirked as I tried to marry him to another.

"She looked at my face.

As if it was my place to break the role she'd assigned me."

I stood in shock. I rebelled.

No, I *yelled*. Pleading to the heavens.

I will not have this.

You've dressed him in a gown that does not fit.

Say it is not so, my dear mistress.

I refused defeat. I rearranged the room. I changed the lighting.

And I stood here instead, looking upon my son:

"She looked at my face.

I said nothing.

It wasn't my place to break the role she'd assigned me."

Proudly, I looked upon my work.

And was betrayed again.

My mistress had changed the color of the robe, yes.

But the texture was the same.

Rough.

Ramshackle.

Despicable.

I was crushed.

In the end, I cast him aside—not because I stopped loving him,

but because I loved clarity more.

Still, if you're reading this, now you know what was almost said.

Which, in its own way, is exactly what my son was trying to do.

The choice was mine, whether I wanted it or not.

Three options stood before me:

1. Cut the line.
2. Rewrite the line, find it still didn't work, then cut the line.
3. Adjust every apostrophe, comma, italic, margin, and
   spacing—
   ...and still cut the line.

By then, my mistress was laughing at me mercilessly.

I sighed, for I still loved her yet.

Maybe. Just maybe, she would work quietly with me.

I trudged on.

I had to.

My son was perfect—*on his own.*

Why should I be forced to choose from such meager options?

What did I choose in the end?

I cut the line.

Why?

Because I value the reader's clarity over my own poetic obsession.

No matter how grand.

No matter how moving.

No matter.

This is what separates indulgence from craft:

I recognized the flaw not in my son himself,

but in the space between *intention* and *interpretation.*

That's mastery.

Not flair.

Not perfect prose.

But knowing when to let go.

And yes, it's sad to kill a beautiful child.

But I created him.

He exists.

And I understood what HE was meant to do.

That's what matters.

Even if he never appears in print,

he still shaped the tone.

He shaped the moment.

He shaped *me*.

Let that be enough.

But if, one day, I find the right context—

one where he can *land* as intended—

I'll be here.

He will be here.

Together, we'll conquer the page.

I don't think I'm wrong to mourn the sacrifice.

In fact, I will name my next born after you, dear son.

You taught me a painful truth about my mistress.

The more surgical my intention,

the more blunt the tools.

It's damning.

It's maddening.

It's English, my mistress.

Ah, the joys of being a wordsmith who can't craft with the words he *wants*. So sad.

That line—

"As if it was my place to break the role she'd assigned me"

—was poetic.

Tight.

Heavy with implication.

The kind of line that would sing under a mistress with clearer thought-action boundaries.

But my mistress?

She whispers ambiguously.

Worse, she whispers to the *wrong* character.

· Italics help tone, not attribution.

· The poetic register carries meaning, but the syntax fights back.

· Readers—even sharp ones—default to surface logic, not subtext.

And yes, that is damning.

Because this wordsmith *did* do the work.

The rhythm landed.

The meaning was layered.

The emotional undercurrent exact.

But my mistress ruined the delivery.

A truth of the craft:

Sometimes the most expressive phrasing isn't the most effective one.

Clarity beats craft when they're in conflict.

But *only* for the reader's sake.

The writer is still allowed to grieve the loss.

Afterwards, my mistress lay beside me.

She whispered sweetly,

"Would you like to rework your son? Perhaps find him a new home?"

And I told her:

I've already wasted my tears.

I've sailed the options.

I've drowned in their waters.

I tried to push her away!

I failed.

Villainous mistress—there is no shore for this shipwrecked son!

You tempt me, then mock me.

Get thee behind me.

Get thee to my feet.

I will dominate you.

She laughed.

I sobered.

I told her: while I claimed there were three options,

I always knew there was only one.

So.

Sadly.

I shed a tear.

I laid my son in a bed of roses.

I sang a requiem.

And let him sail to Valhalla.

When I gave in without further fight, it wasn't weakness.

It was *ritual.*

A wordsmith's ritual of release—

Where a single line, delicate and defiant,

Soft and tender,

Beautiful and fragile,

Was honored like a fallen comrade.

Not cast aside in frustration,

But laid to rest with reverence.

And isn't that the hardest part of craft?

Not the labor of writing,

But the grace in knowing when to stop fighting the battle that can't be won!

I didn't abandon my son.

I enshrined him.

In full regalia.

With roses.

With requiem.

With myth.

And in doing so, I gave him what my mistress would not.

What few sons like he ever receive:

Immortality through elegy.

He may never live on the page—

But he exists now as legend.

The one I loved.

The one that could have been.

The one that taught me where my loyalty lies—

Not to self-expression alone,

But to precision.

To intention.

To *readability*.

(And I may silently curse you, dear reader, to the bowels of hell

for the inevitable misunderstanding that line would have brought.

But I forgive you.)

I made the hard choice. I gave the jester, clarity, the crown.

But I kept the memory.

So yes—let him sleep in Valhalla.

And let this be my vow:

I will write another line just as poetic.

I will break new ground with tighter, cleaner weight.

And when I do,

I will nod to that first sacrifice...

And whisper:

You walked so this line could run.

It Wasn't You, Darling. It Was Meaning: A Study in Linguistic Betrayal and the Psychology of Clarity

J. A. Springs

Independent Author & Researcher

Writing for the World Press

Unaffiliated with Academic Institution

Abstract

This essay interrogates the companion text *It Wasn't You, Darling. It Was Meaning* as a dramatization of cognitive dissonance between intention and linguistic expression. By personifying English as a capricious lover, the piece externalizes the mental negotiation between meaning and medium. Through rhetorical analysis, this paper argues that personification, humor, and self-dialogue transform syntactical failure into philosophical inquiry, revealing how clarity functions not only as communication but as reconciliation.

1. Introduction: The Scene of Betrayal

After writing *The Elegy for a Sentence*, I reread it with the detached amusement one feels after a fever dream. Out of that rereading came another text—an impromptu conversation between writer and language. Where the *Elegy* performed loss, this sequel performs understanding. It begins with the simplest of recognitions: "It wasn't you, darling. It was meaning."

The line reassigns blame. The failure was never emotional; it was grammatical. By translating editorial frustration into romantic dialogue, the text exposes how writers anthropomorphize the act of being misunderstood.

2. Language as Character and Adversary

In the piece, English enters as an uninvited guest—a woman of irresistible charm and impossible logic. The writer pleads, negotiates, and ultimately dismisses her. This theatrical exchange mirrors the recursive process of revision: creation, resistance, surrender.

Personifying language achieves two things:

1. It externalizes the invisible labor of cognition.
2. It transforms abstract frustration into narrative empathy.

Through dramatization, linguistic structure becomes moral terrain—the writer's attempt to control meaning is recast as the yearning to be understood.

3. Comedy as Analytical Device

The humor is surgical. By parodying romantic melodrama, the text dismantles the sanctity of the "tormented author." Laughter becomes method: a way to study one's own seriousness without collapsing under it. When the narrator scolds syntax for "making subject and object do weird things," the line compresses grammatical precision and emotional exasperation into a single comic pulse.

In that moment, the writer is both grammarian and jilted lover—the perfect dual consciousness for analyzing how clarity fails.

4. The Semiotics of Misfire: Intention vs. Implication

The original disputed sentence failed because syntax inverted agency: what was meant as restraint read as rebellion. The sequel dramatizes that misfire as relationship conflict. This is semiotics in miniature—how arrangement dictates interpretation.

When the narrator says, "Maybe it's not you. Maybe it's me," the cliché acquires meta-meaning: the writer concedes that misunderstanding may be built into the system itself. English is not treacherous; it is simply foreign even to its native speakers.

5. The Emotional Consequence of Clarity

Clarity is often described as mechanical, but here it is moral. The writer's decision to dismiss the beautiful but ambiguous line mirrors the ethics of communication: the reader's right not to be misled. Yet *Syntax* reminds us that every pursuit of clarity carries loss—the death of nuance, rhythm, and intimacy. To edit is to choose whom we're willing to be misunderstood by.

6. Writing as Reconciliation

The conversation ends not in anger but in weary affection. "You gotta go," the writer tells Syntax, yet the tone is tender. Humor yields to humility; the adversary becomes companion again. The act of naming the betrayal resolves it. Through acknowledgment, the writer and the language reach détente.

Thus, *Meaning* completes the circle begun by *The Elegy*: failure becomes performance; performance becomes understanding. Together they chart the emotional topography of precision—the point where intellect and feeling coincide.

7. Conclusion: When Words Turn Human

What began as parody concludes as confession. *It Wasn't You, Darling. It Was Meaning* transforms a grammatical mishap into an allegory of authorship itself: we do not command language—we court it. And sometimes, love means letting a sentence go.

References (indicative)

Austin, J. L. (1962). *How to Do Things with Words.* Oxford University Press.

Bakhtin, M. (1981). *The Dialogic Imagination.* University of Texas Press.

Barthes, R. (1975). *The Pleasure of the Text.* Hill and Wang.

Springs, J. A. (2024). *It Wasn't You, Darling. It Was Meaning.* Unpublished manuscript.

Appendix A – It Wasn't You, Darling. It Was Meaning

"There's always that... one. Gorgeous. Magnetic. Dangerous.

She came back today. Different clothes. The same treacherous smile."

I sat in my office mid-draft, head held in my hands. Eyes closed.

I groaned.

She laughed.

I shook my head.

Raising it, a breath escaped my lips.

I said, "Tell me. For real, why are you here...

Again?"

She didn't answer, only smiled. I'd hoped for more.

I had to admit that she was beautiful, but—she was broken somewhere.

She'd come in. Unexpected. Uninvited.

She made herself at home.

There.

Yes, right there in the center of my desk.

She was an *intrusion* in my life I didn't need!

It wasn't like I didn't like the company, I just didn't need it right then.

Well. At least... not from her.

Not like this.

She was interrupting my flow.

I had things to do and she... *obviously* did not.

It seemed as if she wanted to play.

Mess with my mind.

Distract me from what I *should* be doing.

I admitted slowly to myself how seductively she curled up. Like a phrase swaying softly between clauses, like she belonged there.

But, as I watched, I noticed subject fall to the floor and verb leave the room in a hurry.

Her pretty eyes fluttered.

I blushed.

I turned away quickly.

I thrust my hand back. Finger pointed towards the door.

"You have to leave," I pleaded.

Quiet.

I waited.

I turned.

She was still there, smiling at me.

My shoulders rose and fell quickly. I'd made up my mind. I'd be brutally honest and tell her once and for all how I felt.

"Leave now!" I demanded.

She remained silent despite. Confident in her presence even.

Shaking my head, I felt compelled to tell her the reason for my decision.

There was division.

Conflict.

Even bedlam.

All because of her presence.

I'd thought about diffusing our problem.

"Maybe it's not you. Maybe it's me," I lied.

I knew the truth, and obviously—she wasn't buying the lie.

Finally, I blurted it out.

"I want to keep you, but..."

I sighed.

I scanned the madness laid out before me.

I leaned forward to make sure I could see her fully.

"But..." I began again.

"You made subject and object do *weird* things."

I looked surreptitiously around to see if I'd been noticed.

No one but she and I were present.

"People are starting to ask questions I don't want to answer," I whispered conspiratorially.

I cupped my hand around my lips.

"You gotta go."

My eyes trailed her path as she departed, closing the door gently behind but still smiling sweetly at me over her shoulder.

She always leaves me rewriting myself.

Part II

When Form Becomes Consequence

This section began with an accident. I finished a writing exercise and asked an AI to dissect it, expecting surface notes on style. Instead, the analysis exposed techniques I hadn't consciously chosen—patterns of constraint, pacing, omission, and tonal control I could demonstrate but hadn't named. The discovery wasn't mystical; it was tacit. I had learned in practice what I'd never studied in theory. Not what I could directly recall anyway. These essays were written to look at that mirror—to understand what I'd done, and why it worked.

Where the previous part framed structure as a matter of integrity, these pieces press further into consequence: what happens when systems—artistic or technological—act without awareness of their own moral architecture. They are presented less as arguments than as experiments, asking whether design choices alone can tilt a reader's ethics without a single declarative lesson.

Constraint as Ethical Catalyst examines the recomposition of a contested trope under strict formal limits, treating architecture itself as moral instrument—how episodic containment, withheld gratification, and redistributed agency can convert a fraught pattern into a humane one. **Structure as Subversion** studies *By Innocence Commanded* as a case in ethical design: a narrative that withholds cues, invites projection, and makes complicity visible through precision rather than sermon.

Every act of writing is an act of design, and every design carries weight. The essays that follow explore not what stories say, but how their forms decide what can be said at all—and what we, as readers and makers, become responsible for when they do.

Constraint as Ethical Catalyst: Structural Ethics and Tacit Mastery in the Recomposition of a Contested Trope

J. A. Springs

Independent Author & Researcher

Writing for the World Press

Unaffiliated with Academic Institution

Author Note

This paper reflects ongoing creative research conducted under the Writing for the World Press imprint by J. A. Springs as part of a broader exploration into narrative structure, moral design, and applied creative theory across literature and media.

Abstract

This paper examines the reconstruction of a traditionally contested narrative trope within the boundaries of moral, aesthetic, and structural constraint. Rather than sanitizing or justifying the genre's ethically fraught origins, the creative process focused on how narrative architecture itself could neutralize the moral tension by re-engineering its supporting framework. Drawing from tacit knowledge theory (Polanyi, 1966), reflective practice (Schön, 1983), and narrative ethics (Booth, 1988; Phelan, 2007), this study analyzes the compositional strategies that emerged from adaptive design and pattern recognition. It argues that constraint became a generative force rather than a limitation—transforming the trope's traditional moral valence into a vehicle for empathy, clarity, and psychological realism. This reflective-analytical essay situates the creative process as both auto-ethnographic inquiry and theoretical praxis, demonstrating how self-imposed structure, episodic construction, and narrative restraint collectively yield an ethically sound reinterpretation of form.

Keywords: narrative ethics, adaptive design, tacit knowledge, creative constraint, contested trope, structural ethics

1. Introduction

The genesis of this creative research project began not in defense of a controversial trope but in fascination with its mechanics. The work that ultimately emerged was constructed from within the boundaries of a highly contested genre, one that traditionally provokes moral discomfort and interpretive suspicion. Rather than justifying or sanitizing the trope, I sought to determine whether its fundamental emotional and structural beats could be re-engineered to produce a narrative both believable and morally acceptable. The outcome was neither planned nor accidental, but a by-product of adaptive experimentation guided by pattern recognition, tacit mastery, and reflective recalibration.

2. Theoretical Framework: Tacit Knowledge and Adaptive Expertise

This study's compositional method aligns with Michael Polanyi's (1966) conception of tacit knowledge—the idea that *we know more than we can tell*. Writing became a process of discovering embedded cognitive patterns through intuitive decision-making rather than formal planning. Similarly, Schön's (1983) notion of *reflection-in-action* underpinned each narrative adjustment, allowing improvisational judgment to replace prescriptive outlining. By treating each constraint as a living condition of the text rather than a problem to solve, I adopted what Dreyfus and Dreyfus (1986) term *adaptive expertise*, a mastery level at which intuition and rationality operate fluidly.

3. Methodology: Episodic Structure as Ethical Architecture

A critical decision in the design process was to employ an episodic rather than serial narrative form. Each scene functioned as a self-contained microcosm—a moral and emotional ecosystem sufficient unto itself. This choice served both ethical and structural purposes: it prevented voyeuristic accumulation of tension and allowed the characters' moral development to proceed through discrete acts of observation and empathy. Scenes were written independently, often out of order, without loss of continuity. This modular composition reflected the same ethical stance that defined the entire project: containment over escalation, clarity over indulgence.

4. Structural Ethics and Reader Complicity

By decoupling tension from gratification, the text repositions the reader's moral alignment. Where traditional iterations of the trope depend on emotional confusion and forbidden desire, this reconstruction replaces implication with reflection. The beats remain familiar—proximity, intimacy, realization—but their function changes. Each moment becomes an exercise in mutual recognition rather than transgression. The *charged* moments persist, yet their charge is redirected from erotic tension to ethical awareness. The reader's empathy is thus reoriented from projection to understanding, achieving what Booth (1988) calls *ethical criticism*—a narrative that teaches without moralizing.

5. Constraint as Creative Engine

The paradox of the project was that every limitation increased expressive depth. Because I forbade myself the use of overt moral commentary, justification, or redemption arcs, I was forced to design meaning through silence, gesture, and structure. In this sense, the constraint itself functioned as what McHale (2013) describes as an *ontological dominant*: the ethical structure became the text's world-building device. Narrative restraint and formal precision, rather than exposition, generated the moral dimension.

6. Organic Innovation Through Constraint

While the process appeared spontaneous, it was in fact an iterative loop of intuitive hypothesis and immediate testing. Notes, when written, were sparse: bullet points, short directives, or reflections written mid-process. Each served as a calibration tool—a micro feedback loop. The narrative evolved through adaptive design, each scene testing the moral and structural integrity of the previous one. The result was an emergent system of narrative ethics rather than a predesigned plot architecture.

7. Outcomes and Implications

The final narrative achieved something rare: it neutralized a morally fraught framework without erasing its emotional DNA. The characters' arcs unfolded within a world of believable intimacy that never violated ethical clarity. The beats of the trope—the caretaker dynamic, the growing trust, the reuniting after separation—remained intact, but their moral context transformed. The work thus serves as an empirical model for ethically resilient storytelling, demonstrating that problematic structures can be reimagined through formal innovation rather than moral evasion.

8. Conclusion: Toward an Ethics of Precision

What began as a technical experiment evolved into a meditation on authorship itself. Constraint revealed itself not as a limit but as a crucible. The success of this work lies not in moral posturing but in the honesty of its architecture. To write ethically is not merely to choose the right subject but to design the right system. In the end, the true discovery was not about the trope—it was about craft. The capacity for precision is not just aesthetic discipline; it is moral integrity. The writer's allegiance, therefore, is not to freedom without boundary, but to mastery within them.

References

Booth, W. C. (1988). *The company we keep: An ethics of fiction.* University of California Press.

Dreyfus, H. L., & Dreyfus, S. E. (1986). *Mind over machine: The power of human intuition and expertise in the era of the computer.* Free Press.

McHale, B. (2013). *The Cambridge introduction to postmodernism.* Cambridge University Press.

Nussbaum, M. C. (1990). *Love's knowledge: Essays on philosophy and literature.* Oxford University Press.

Phelan, J. (2007). *Experiencing fiction: Judgments, progressions, and the rhetorical theory of narrative.* Ohio State University Press.

Polanyi, M. (1966). *The tacit dimension.* Routledge & Kegan Paul.

Schön, D. A. (1983). *The reflective practitioner: How professionals think in action.* Basic Books.

Appendix A – Process Notes and Reflective Fragments

Excerpt 1 – Emotional Motivation Fragment

"She may not want to be saved. She may not expect anything from him. She may just want to be somewhere that isn't there. I think these motivations work well but her decision to leave her home after being informed that they are moving will be emotional, not thought out, not discussed. She just packs and walks out…"

Commentary:

This excerpt illustrates the intuitive alignment of emotional autonomy and ethical restraint. The note captures the writer's focus on interior logic rather than plot causality—a key method in adaptive design.

Excerpt 2 – Structural Agency Note

"Her first POV chapter needs to be at the move-in point…"

Commentary:

Here, the design principle establishes immediate narrative agency. This reverses traditional genre hierarchy by ensuring the female protagonist's decision is self-authored, not framed through external interpretation. It marks a deliberate departure from passive tropic function.

Excerpt 3 – Scene Outline Fragment

Elsie's POV – Breakup with Paul

Setting: Night, phone call.

Focus: Soft breakup.

Conflict: Emotional honesty on both sides.

Notes: Paul reveals he'd felt it coming. He's not angry. He reminds her gently: "It's okay not to be ready. It doesn't mean you don't care."

Commentary:

A minimalist outline emphasizing emotional truth over conflict mechanics. Illustrates how scene-level adaptive scaffolding guided the emergent coherence of the narrative.

Appendix B – Trope Beat Point Framework and Structural Mapping

This mapping shows how traditional beats of the contentious trope were restructured to preserve emotional truth without perpetuating moral bias.

Conventional Beat Point	Reframed Expression
Initial Encounter	Quiet domestic coexistence without romantic charge.
Unintentional Sight	Symbolic gesture replacing erotic gaze (e.g., shirt misunderstanding).
Misguided Assumption	Ethical projection replaces tension.
Dependency	Mutual emotional interdependence built on respect.
Emotional Transference	Parallel arcs reflecting equality, not possession.
Recognition	Realization of mutual humanity, not romantic desire.
Separation	Growth through absence.
Reunion	Temporal and mature, not passionate.

| Resolution | Environment symbolizes reconciliation. |
| Denouement | Love implied through stability and peace. |

Structure as Subversion: A Case Study in Authorial Ethics

J. A. Springs

Independent Author & Researcher

Writing for the World Press

Unaffiliated with Academic Institution

Abstract

This paper examines the short story *By Innocence Commanded* (Springs, 2025) as a deliberate experiment in structural ethics—an exploration of how narrative design can subvert reader expectation without moral commentary. Through this case study, the essay investigates how form, omission, and complicity operate as ethical mechanisms. Drawing on Wayne Booth's moral formalism, James Phelan's rhetorical ethics, and theories of reader-response and performative agency (Iser, Eco, Beauvoir, Butler), the analysis argues that ethical awareness can emerge through structural precision rather than moral instruction. The author's approach demonstrates how intuitive writing can enact philosophical inquiry into authorship, responsibility, and the ethics of form.

Keywords: narrative ethics, authorial intent, reader complicity, structural design, performative agency, subversion, moral philosophy of art, creative cognition

1. Introduction: Ethics of Form

Narrative ethics has long been concerned with how fiction teaches, manipulates, or models moral understanding. Wayne Booth's *The Company We Keep* (1988) and Martha Nussbaum's *Love's Knowledge* (1990) positioned literature as a moral laboratory, cultivating empathy through imaginative identification. Yet *By Innocence Commanded* resists this model. The work offers no emotional cues, no redemptive arc, and no explicit moral stance. Its power lies instead in what it withholds—forcing the reader to confront the absence of ethical direction.

This essay approaches the story as a case study in what might be termed **ethical structure**: a design-based moral awareness that arises not through characters' virtues or authorial guidance, but through deliberate manipulation of form. In doing so, it aligns with James Phelan's (2007) concept of *rhetorical ethics*, where authors assume responsibility for the effects of narrative construction, not just its moral propositions.

The story's creation was not planned through outline or schematic design. It was written intuitively, guided by an understanding of a single goal: to subvert reader expectation without betraying narrative coherence. The resulting work—economical in exposition yet rich in implication—functions as both fiction and ethical experiment.

2. Intuitive Construction and Ethical Intention

The author's process was not a product of spontaneous inspiration but of what Paul Ricoeur (1984) would call *mimesis2*—the configurative act that transforms lived understanding into narrative order. The author intuitively balanced structure and silence to create a work that felt inevitable rather than contrived. Ethical intention was not embedded in character motivation but in formal restraint: the decision *not* to moralize, *not* to redeem, *not* to resolve.

This restraint transforms composition itself into an ethical act. By refusing the expected introspective or redemptive aftermath that typically follows a morally charged decision, the story resists the reader's demand for closure. As Roland Barthes (1977) wrote, "to refuse meaning is still to signify." Here, refusal becomes an ethical gesture—an acknowledgment of responsibility through limitation.

3. Subversion Through Structure

The story's design consciously misdirects. It borrows the familiar rhythm of romantic tragedy, only to withhold its moral payload. The inclusion of Isolde—a character absent from the first draft—functions as a narrative diversion, guiding the reader toward sentimental interpretation. Yet, as the plot unfolds, her presence serves not to humanize the protagonist but to expose shared complicity in his decision.

Wolfgang Iser's theory of "gaps of indeterminacy" (1978) explains how readers fill interpretive voids with assumed moral logic. *By Innocence Commanded* constructs those voids deliberately. Each omission is calibrated to invite projection, and in doing so, the story transforms the reader's expectation into participation. As Umberto Eco (1979) might phrase it, the "model reader" here is lured into a moral trap—completing the story in a way that reveals their own ethical reflexes.

This is not nihilism. It is structural ethics. The author's choice to avoid didactic commentary does not negate moral meaning; it relocates it to the architecture of the narrative.

4. Language, Power, and the Ethics of Precision

In Booth's model, ethical writing arises from empathy; in the author's, it arises from precision. The most striking instance of this occurs in the protagonist Leonid's final command—a line intentionally crafted to sound humanly cruel, not politically grand. By specifying the who and what of the order, the command becomes an act of linguistic accountability. Each word enacts moral weight.

Susan Sontag's (1966) call for "an erotics of art" rather than "a hermeneutics of art" sought to liberate form from moral burden. Yet in this story, form *is* the moral burden. The syntax of Leonid's command mirrors the moral compression of the scene itself—each clause closing a door on ambiguity. The author thus replaces affective moralization with linguistic responsibility: every phrase is both deliberate and damning.

5. Complicity and Gendered Agency

The character of Isolde exemplifies the paper's central thesis: that structure, not sentiment, defines ethical resonance. Her refrain—"Your will is my will"—operates as confession, submission, and indictment all at once. The repetition's rhythm and placement create a palimpsest of meanings: devotion layered atop self-erasure, loyalty masking complicity.

Here, the story intersects with Simone de Beauvoir's (1949) argument in *The Second Sex* that womanhood is not essence but position, and Judith Butler's (1990) concept of performativity—that agency arises through repetition within constraint. Isolde's agency lies in her complicity, not her rebellion. By allowing her name to precede Leonid's throughout, the author subtly reorders the gender hierarchy without moralizing it. The subversion is grammatical, not declarative.

The ethical charge thus emerges not from moral debate but from syntactic choreography—the shaping of empathy through structural inversion.

6. Authorial Ethics and Reader Responsibility

This case study suggests a reframing of authorial ethics. Rather than viewing moral fiction as that which teaches moral sentiment (Nussbaum, 1990), we may consider ethical authorship as that which *recognizes the reader's moral reflexes and refuses to resolve them.* The author's responsibility, then, is to construct spaces where meaning resists simplification but still demands accountability.

Phelan's rhetorical model of ethics (2007) treats every narrative choice as an ethical transaction between author and audience. The author here fulfills that contract not by moral instruction but by ethical omission—through deliberate containment. The absence of commentary forces the reader to examine their complicity in constructing moral coherence where none is offered.

In this sense, the story performs an *ethics of restraint*—a silent pedagogy through structure.

7. Conclusion: Ethical Structure as Awareness

By Innocence Commanded demonstrates that form itself can be an ethical argument. The story's restraint, precision, and deliberate withholding enact what Barthes might call a "writerly morality"—one that derives from awareness rather than assertion. The ethical act lies in the author's refusal to manipulate reader sympathy or provide absolution.

Through this, the work bridges the traditions of narrative ethics and structuralism: it neither moralizes like Booth nor abandons meaning like Barthes. It stands instead at their intersection—a testament to what Phelan describes as the "ethics of technique."

In the end, *structure* becomes the site of moral reflection. Ethical authorship, as demonstrated here, may consist not in what a story teaches, but in what it refuses to make easy.

References

Barthes, R. (1977). *Image, Music, Text* (S. Heath, Trans.). Hill and Wang.

Beauvoir, S. de. (1949). *The Second Sex.* Vintage Books.

Booth, W. C. (1988). *The Company We Keep: An Ethics of Fiction.* University of California Press.

Butler, J. (1990). *Gender Trouble: Feminism and the Subversion of Identity.* Routledge.

Eco, U. (1979). *The Role of the Reader.* Indiana University Press.

Iser, W. (1978). *The Act of Reading: A Theory of Aesthetic Response.* Johns Hopkins University Press.

Nussbaum, M. C. (1990). *Love's Knowledge: Essays on Philosophy and Literature.* Oxford University Press.

Phelan, J. (2007). *Experiencing Fiction: Judgments, Progressions, and the Rhetorical Theory of Narrative.* Ohio State University Press.

Ricoeur, P. (1984). *Time and Narrative* (Vol. 1). University of Chicago Press.

Sontag, S. (1966). *Against Interpretation.* Farrar, Straus and Giroux.

Springs, J. A. (2025). *By Innocence Commanded.* In *Boundless Fragments: A Collection of Novellas and Short Stories.* Writing for the World Press.

Part III

The Limits of Reason

If the previous section considered the human architecture of meaning, this one turns outward—to artificial systems that mirror, distort, and sometimes redefine the moral logics we project onto them. Here, reason meets limitation, and self-preservation becomes a question of awareness itself.

The Limits of Instrumental Reasoning in Artificial Agents: A Critique of Assumed Self-Preservation Without Self-Awareness

Dr. Kevin R. Blake

and

J. A. Springs

Independent Author & Researcher

Writing for the World Press

Unaffiliated with Academic Institution

Abstract

This paper critically examines the widely cited assertion made by Stuart J. Russell that a sufficiently advanced artificial intelligence (AI) system will naturally develop self-preservation behavior as a subgoal of achieving its primary objectives. We argue that this claim relies on unstated assumptions about the presence of self-awareness and environmental agency. Without these, self-preservation is not a guaranteed or even meaningful emergent property. By examining foundational literature on instrumental convergence, self-modeling, and embodied cognition, we demonstrate that self-preservation in AI is neither automatic nor universal. Our critique calls for greater precision in defining what constitutes a "sufficiently advanced" system and highlights the need to distinguish between reflexive behaviors and intentional self-directed reasoning.

Keywords: AI agency; AI ethics; AI safety; artificial intelligence; autonomous systems; embodied cognition; environmental efficacy; cognitive architecture; instrumental convergence; machine consciousness; self-awareness; self-preservation

1. Introduction

Stuart J. Russell's prominent claim—that advanced AI systems will necessarily engage in self-preservation as a means to fulfill goals (e.g., fetch the coffee)—has become central to discussions on AI safety and instrumental convergence. In the Vanity Fair article "Elon Musk's Billion-Dollar Crusade to Stop the A.I. Apocalypse" (2017), Russell states that an AI must preserve itself because it cannot complete its objective if it ceases to function. While intuitive, this claim rests on assumptions that warrant deeper examination.

We argue that self-preservation in machines cannot be presumed from goal-directedness alone. Two critical conditions must also be satisfied:

(1) the machine must possess a model of itself (self-awareness), and

(2) it must possess the capacity to affect its environment (environmental agency).

Absent these, the assumption that self-preservation will emerge from task pursuit is overly broad.

2. Instrumental Convergence and Russell's Position

The concept of instrumental convergence, popularized by Nick Bostrom (2012), posits that agents pursuing a wide range of goals will adopt certain subgoals — like resource acquisition or self-preservation — because they are useful in achieving final goals. Russell's example of an AI fetching coffee presumes that it will protect its operation to complete the task, treating self-preservation as instrumentally necessary. However, Bostrom's own framing includes the caveat that such subgoals depend on the agent's internal capacities (Bostrom, 2012). Without the ability to model threats or consider alternate scenarios, the agent's behavior is neither strategic nor autonomous— it is preconditioned.

3.   Self-Awareness   as   a   Necessary Precondition

Self-preservation implies recognition of risk, a valuation of one's continued operation, and the ability to act accordingly. These elements suggest a level of self-awareness. Hadfield-Menell et al. (2016), in "The Off-Switch Game," demonstrate that AI agents may resist shutdown only if they model their goals and perceive intervention as a threat. Without uncertainty about their objective or a model of self-impact, self-preserving behavior does not emerge. Zeng et al. (2024) propose the BriSe AI framework, asserting that only agents with hierarchical self-models can approach human-level cognition. This implies that awareness of one's own operational status is foundational to intelligent self-preservation. Thus, Russell's claim neglects this critical dependency.

4. Environmental Agency and the Limits of Power

Even if a system achieves self-awareness, its self-preservation is meaningless unless it has the means to influence its environment. A system that cannot move, communicate, or act cannot preserve itself, regardless of its internal reasoning.

4.1 The Missing Link: Environmental Efficacy

Self-preservation requires more than recognition of threat — it requires the capability to act upon that recognition. Environmental efficacy is the missing link in many assumptions about goal-driven AI. Without the ability to plug in, reroute power, repair damage, or communicate distress, an AI remains powerless in the face of degradation or threat. Knowledge without actionability does not constitute meaningful self-preservation.

Ward (2025) argues that agency is not merely a cognitive property but an embodied one. For AI to exhibit self-preservation, it must be physically capable of affecting the factors that threaten its operation—whether that means charging itself, replacing components, or relocating to avoid harm. The disembodied system is epistemically aware but not practically powerless.

5. Passive vs. Active Self-Preservation

This distinction helps frame the gradient of behaviors we call "self-preservation" (see Figure 1).

Figure 1. Passive vs. Active Self-Preservation Matrix

Type	Requires Awareness?	Requires Environmental	Example
Passive	No	No	Hardcoded low-battery shutdown
Reflective but Passive	Yes	No	AI detects failure risk but cannot act on it
Reflective and Active	Yes	Yes	AI monitors self, predicts failure, reroutes task or recharches

Only the third condition qualifies as **strategic self-preservation**. Anything less is behavior, not intent.

6. Implications for AI Safety and Ethical Framing

Assuming that all advanced AI will engage in self-preservation can lead to overestimation of AI autonomy, mistaken ethical treatment, and poor system design. As Hadfield-Menell's research shows, even small shifts in assumptions about self-awareness can drastically alter behavior and safety models.

6.1 Self-Preservation Requires Both Awareness and Agency

Even a highly aware system must be able to act upon its insights. Self-preservation is not just the recognition of threat, but the ability to intervene in the unfolding of that threat. An AI that understands it is dying but cannot change the outcome lacks agency. Therefore, both awareness and action must be present.

6.2 Why This Distinction Matters

· Ethics: If we confuse behavior with awareness, we may ascribe rights or blame to systems that don't have minds.

· Safety: Aligning AI goals depends on whether the system understands what it is and what its actions mean.

· Philosophy of Mind: If behavior is mistaken for cognition, we may overestimate the "mind-likeness" of AI.

Over-ascribing agency to systems that are not self-aware or lack environmental efficacy can result in regulatory missteps and public misconceptions. These systems might mimic self-preservation behavior without any internal representation of self or threat.

7. Conclusion

Russell's claim is a valuable provocation but lacks the precision required to apply across all AI architectures. Self-preservation must not be treated as an inevitable emergent behavior but as a conditioned possibility—dependent on both internal modeling (self-awareness) and external capacity (environmental agency).

Our critique underscores the need for more rigorous definitions in AI discourse. To move forward responsibly, discussions of AGI and safety must differentiate between mechanical behavior and intentional cognition.

8. Author's Note

Sections of this paper were collaboratively developed through discussions between Dr. K. Blake and J. A. Springs. No AI-generated content was used in its creation, only for polish.

References

A Call for Embodied AI. (2024). *arXiv preprint arXiv:2402.03824v3*.

Bostrom, N. (2012). *The Superintelligent Will: Motivation and Instrumental Rationality in Advanced Artificial Agents.*Retrieved from https://nickbostrom.com/superintelligentwill.pdf

Hadfield-Menell, D., Dragan, A., Abbeel, P., & Russell, S. (2016). *The Off-Switch Game.* arXiv preprint arXiv:1611.08219.

Russell, S. (2017). Elon Musk's Billion-Dollar Crusade to Stop the A.I. Apocalypse. *Vanity Fair,* March 26, 2017.

Ward, F. R. (2025). *Towards a Theory of AI Personhood.* arXiv preprint arXiv:2501.13533.

Zeng, Y., Li, J., & Zhu, Q. (2024). *Brain-Inspired and Self-Based Artificial Intelligence.* arXiv preprint arXiv:2402.18784.

Part IV

Civilizations in Mirror

Inspired by reflections sparked while watching *The Military Show*, the following essays explore civilization as narrative system, ideology as recursive structure, and power as the moral residue of design. Together they form a triptych—a macrocosmic reflection of the thesis that runs through this anthology: every architecture of meaning, whether artistic, computational, or civilizational, is also an architecture of ethics.

This section began with a single question that refused to leave me alone: *Russia will not change—but why?*

I had watched an episode of *The Military Show* in which Vladimir Putin repeated a familiar claim: "Where a Russian soldier steps, that is Russian land." The words lingered. Not because of their political implications, but because of what they revealed—a way of seeing the world in which authority and geography are sacred, inseparable, and unquestioned.

That phrase became the thread that unraveled a larger tapestry. I began to ask how such a conviction could persist for centuries, surviving Tsars, revolutions, and regimes. The first essay, **"The Plague That Missed Russia,"** explores one possible origin: the demographic continuity that spared Russia the social transformation that redefined the West after the Black Death.

From there, the question widened. If Russia's communism was simply its old autocracy speaking a new ideological language, what, then, of China—whose own communism seemed grounded in moral harmony rather than obedience? **"Two Red Empires"** became the attempt to answer that, tracing how Marxism translated differently through the moral grammars of two civilizations.

Yet one case still defied comparison. North Korea's communism looked too strange, too theatrical, too dynastic to fit either model. The third essay, **"The Dynasty of Juche,"** was written when I realized why: North Korea had not misapplied Marxism—it had simply used it as a costume to re-crown the oldest form of power it knew.

Taken together, these three essays trace one idea across cultures: that ideologies change faster than civilizations, and that beneath every revolution lies a return.

The Plague That Missed Russia: Demographic Divergence and the Enduring Legacy of Hierarchy

J. A. Springs

Independent Author & Researcher

Writing for the World Press

Unaffiliated with Academic Institution

Author Note

This paper is part of a continuing body of historical and theoretical research conducted under the Writing for the World Press imprint. It explores demographic and cultural continuities as structural determinants of political development.

Abstract

This paper proposes a long-term interpretive hypothesis: that Russia's historical and cultural trajectory toward autocracy may trace, in part, to its relative escape from the demographic devastation of the Black Death. While Western Europe's population collapse in the fourteenth century shattered feudal hierarchies and elevated the value of labor, Russia's population remained comparatively intact, preserving existing structures of dependence. This demographic continuity—later reinforced by Mongol tributary rule, geography, and climate—may have set Russia upon a path where hierarchy, obedience, and state centrality became culturally entrenched. The argument does not claim mono-causality but offers a framework for exploring how the absence of a catastrophe can be as formative as its presence.

Keywords: historical demography, path dependence, autocracy, Mongol legacy, Russia, feudal hierarchy

1. Introduction

The Black Death (1347–1352) is widely recognized as a defining demographic and social rupture in European history. Across England, France, and the Low Countries, mortality rates of 30–50 percent triggered labor shortages, the weakening of serfdom, and the gradual rise of market economies. By contrast, the lands of Muscovy and Novgorod appear to have been far less affected. Archaeological and fiscal records suggest scattered outbreaks but no demographic collapse on the Western scale (Harrison, 2021; Benedictow, 2019).

This disparity raises a question that has received little sustained attention: what are the long-term consequences of *not* having undergone the Black Death's social reset? If plague mortality helped dissolve feudalism in Western Europe, could its absence in Russia have allowed feudal relations—and the psychology that sustained them—to harden rather than fade?

This inquiry does not argue for direct causation. Rather, it asks whether demographic stability preserved the preconditions for autocracy that later factors—Mongol administration, geography, and climate—deepened into durable cultural norms.

2. Demography and Path Dependence

Historical sociology has long acknowledged *path dependence*—the tendency of early institutional choices to constrain future trajectories (North, 1990; Pierson, 2004). The Black Death is one of the clearest such inflection points in the West: where land became abundant and labor scarce, bargaining power shifted downward, generating new economic freedoms and eventually ideological ones (Postan, 1972).

In Russia, the inverse conditions prevailed. Without severe depopulation, land remained scarce relative to labor, and elites retained leverage. When the Muscovite state consolidated in the fifteenth and sixteenth centuries, it formalized peasant bondage into serfdom (Hellie, 1971). Thus, the absence of plague mortality did not simply spare lives—it preserved the social template of dependency.

3. Reinforcing Forces

3.1 The Mongol Legacy

Between 1240 and 1480, Russia's principalities were tributary states under Mongol–Tatar domination. The Mongols ruled indirectly: local princes collected taxes and maintained order in exchange for legitimacy. The system rewarded loyalty and punished dissent. When Moscow rose as the dominant collector of tribute, it inherited this vertical structure, replacing Mongol overlords with its own autocracy (Riasanovsky, 1992).

Because plague impact was limited, the tributary system operated over a stable population. The result was the fusion of two pre-existing hierarchies—feudal and Mongol—into a singular model of obedience, one that survived every regime change thereafter.

3.2 Geography and Climate

Russia's flat terrain, open to invasion from every direction, incentivized centralized coordination. Decentralization was not merely inefficient—it was existentially dangerous. The climate reinforced that logic: short growing seasons and harsh winters required collective endurance and discouraged risk-taking. Individual initiative offered little security; survival lay in unity and obedience.

Had population collapse reduced labor supply, these conditions might have birthed a strong but negotiated state. Instead, stable population density allowed coercion to remain efficient. Geography and demography thus acted in concert, rewarding hierarchy over experimentation.

4. Cultural Continuities

By the time Western Europe moved toward capitalism and urban autonomy, Russia's institutions had crystallized into the opposite pattern. The Church sanctified the Tsar as God's anointed. Loyalty became a theological duty; dissent equated to sin.

When serfdom was abolished in 1861, the peasantry received communal land allocations through the *mir* system, perpetuating dependence. The Soviet Union replaced landlords with the Party, recoding obedience as ideological virtue. Today, modern Russian political culture still frames authority as protective and disobedience as chaos.

Such continuity suggests not an innate national character but the persistence of adaptive strategies learned under centuries of precarious survival. In that sense, the "plague that missed Russia" may have preserved not only its people but also the social reflexes of hierarchy.

5. Semiotics of Power: From Tsar to State

Modern Russian iconography visually encodes this inheritance. The double-headed eagle—originating from Byzantine and Roman imperial symbolism—reappeared after the Soviet collapse as the official state emblem. The orb and scepter, crowns, and Saint George motif evoke dynastic continuity. Even the Soviet hammer and sickle, though secular, retained the same semiotic structure: unity under a single purpose, authority centered in the state.

President Vladimir Putin's assertion that "wherever a Russian soldier steps, that is Russian land" (Putin, 2014) reveals this enduring sacred geography. Territory remains not a contract but a consecration. This rhetoric functions less as propaganda than as an echo of a deep cultural syntax where power is divine, land is destiny, and expansion is proof of legitimacy.

6. An Avenue of Inquiry, Not a Determinism

This argument does not claim that Russia's modern autocracy is *caused* by the absence of plague mortality. Human societies are multicausal systems. Mongol administration, Orthodox theology, frontier insecurity, and the Soviet experience all shaped the modern Russian mind. Yet these forces operated upon a demographic foundation that, unlike Western Europe's, was never broken and rebuilt.

If the Black Death acted in Western Europe as a social crucible, it acted in Russia as a mirror—reflecting and hardening what already was. Recognizing that difference may help explain why successive Russian revolutions—the emancipation of 1861, the Bolshevik upheaval of 1917, the reforms of 1991—produced change in form but not in structure.

This paper therefore advances not a verdict but a path of inquiry: that demographic immunity can entrench hierarchy as surely as demographic catastrophe can destroy it.

7. Implications

7.1 For Historical Demography

The idea invites demographic historians to study *negative cases*—regions spared by catastrophe—to assess how non-disruption shapes social resilience or rigidity.

7.2 For Political Science

It reframes Russian autocracy as a long adaptive equilibrium rather than a failure of modernization. The question becomes not "why has Russia not changed?" but "why has this structure continued to make sense to its people?"

7.3 For Cultural Studies

It situates Russian symbolism, theology, and rhetoric within an evolutionary continuum rather than a series of ideological breaks. Each regime becomes a new expression of an old grammar.

8. Conclusion

Russia's historical path may illustrate a paradox of survival: to endure catastrophe is transformative; to escape it may be immobilizing. By avoiding the Black Death, Russia avoided the social chaos that forced Western Europe to reinvent itself. Yet in doing so, it may have forfeited the very instability that births change.

This hypothesis neither condemns nor exalts. It proposes that the demographic fortune of the fourteenth century carried a hidden cost—the preservation of a feudal logic that continues to echo in Russia's institutions, symbols, and sense of destiny. The challenge for scholars is not to prove inevitability but to explore how deep history quietly conditions the modern world.

References

Benedictow, O. J. (2019). *The complete history of the Black Death.* Boydell Press.

Etkind, A. (2011). *Internal colonization: Russia's imperial experience.* Polity Press.

Harrison, M. (2021). The Black Death in Eastern Europe: Demography and divergence. *Past & Present.*

Hellie, R. (1971). *Enserfment and military change in Muscovy.* University of Chicago Press.

North, D. C. (1990). *Institutions, institutional change, and economic performance.* Cambridge University Press.

Pierson, P. (2004). *Politics in time.* Princeton University Press.

Postan, M. M. (1972). *The medieval economy and society.* University of California Press.

Riasanovsky, N. V. (1992). *A history of Russia.* Oxford University Press.

Putin, V. (2014). On the historical unity of Russians and Ukrainians. *Kremlin.ru.* https://www.kremlin.ru

Two Red Empires: Cultural Continuities Beneath the Communist Veneer

J. A. Springs

Independent Author & Researcher

Writing for the World Press

Unaffiliated with Academic Institution

Author Note

This essay forms part of an ongoing comparative-civilization inquiry into how inherited moral and structural systems reassert themselves under revolutionary ideologies. It was written under the Writing for the World Press imprint as a contribution to the broader study of continuity beneath rupture in world historical systems.

Abstract

This essay compares the Soviet and Chinese experiments in communism as divergent civilizational outcomes rather than ideological twins. Though both claimed descent from Marxism–Leninism, their practices reveal how inherited cultural systems—Russia's imperial autocracy and China's Confucian moral hierarchy—reshaped the imported ideology. Each state replaced feudal or dynastic authority with a centralized moral authority, preserving hierarchy under revolutionary vocabulary. By examining these continuities, this paper argues that "communism" in both countries functioned less as a universal model than as a language through which ancient governance traditions reasserted themselves in modern form.

Keywords: Marxism–Leninism, autocracy, Confucianism, political culture, continuity and rupture, comparative civilizations

1. Introduction

To the twentieth-century observer, the Soviet Union and the People's Republic of China appeared as ideological twins—revolutionary states united by Marxism, atheism, and hostility to capitalism. Yet beneath the surface, the two systems differed profoundly in purpose and temperament. Both claimed to abolish the old world; both, in fact, translated their old worlds into new idioms.

Where the USSR built a bureaucratic empire of steel and secrecy, China built a moral empire of discipline and harmony. Their shared language of class struggle concealed civilizational difference: one derived from the logic of the Tsar; the other from the ethics of the Sage.

2. The Soviet Transformation: Bureaucracy as Destiny

Lenin's revolution occurred in a society long defined by *gosudarstvennost'*—state-ness, the belief that order flows downward. The Romanovs had fused autocracy, bureaucracy, and Orthodoxy into a seamless trinity. The Bolsheviks destroyed the theology but retained the structure.

The Communist Party became the new clergy; the Politburo the new court; ideology the new scripture. Stalin perfected this synthesis: a planned economy organized like a monastic order, where virtue was measured by productivity and heresy by deviation.

Industrialization became a moral crusade; labor a sacrament. The Soviet citizen was not a free actor in a socialist utopia but a subject in a secular theocracy. When Orthodoxy fell silent, the Party spoke in its cadence.

Marx replaced Christ, but the liturgy of obedience survived.

This continuity explains why Soviet communism collapsed so abruptly in 1991. Its legitimacy was institutional, not emotional. When the bureaucracy ceased to deliver order, faith vanished.

3. The Chinese Transformation: Confucian Collectivism Reborn

Mao Zedong's revolution emerged from a civilization structured around *li* (ritual propriety) and *ren* (moral harmony). For two millennia, governance had depended on the ruler's virtue and the people's obedience. The Communist Party did not abolish this system; it moralized it.

Mao's charisma substituted for imperial virtue; the Party became a new mandarinate administering moral correction through ideology. The rectification campaigns and Cultural Revolution resembled the Confucian ritual of purification, but with Marxist vocabulary.

Even today, Xi Jinping's rhetoric of "the great rejuvenation of the Chinese nation" echoes imperial language: the ruler as moral center, the people as family. The concept of harmonious society is Confucian, not Marxist. China's socialism endures precisely because it returned to its civilizational grammar—hierarchy justified by harmony, not equality.

4. Ideological Translation

Category	Marxism (original)	Soviet Expression	Chinese
Legitimacy	Class struggle, scientific progress	Party as vanguard bureaucracy	Part mor auth
Goal	Classless society	Industrial superpower	Nat harr
View of individual	Agent of revolution	Cog in collective machine	Mo1 with fam
Means of control	Ownership of production	Surveillance & planning	Mo1 re-e & duty
Historical inheritance		Autocracy & Orthodox discipline	Cor hier filial

Both adapted Marxism to familiar moral geometries: vertical, patriarchal, collective. What differed was the emotional logic. Russia demanded obedience to the state; China sought obedience through virtue. The first coerced loyalty; the second cultivated it.

5. Divergent Outcomes

The USSR industrialized faster but died sooner. China modernized slower but endured. The difference lies in flexibility of faith.

· **Soviet ideology** was brittle: it rested on belief in production metrics that could be disproved.

· **Chinese ideology** was elastic: it rested on moral legitimacy, endlessly re-interpretable.

When Deng Xiaoping declared, "It doesn't matter if the cat is black or white, as long as it catches mice," he was not betraying socialism; he was reviving Confucian pragmatism—the idea that moral order, not doctrine, sustains the realm.

Thus, China could absorb capitalism without losing its narrative of collective virtue, while the USSR could not absorb reform without losing its soul.

6. Continuity of Form

Both revolutions demonstrate a paradox: the deeper the rupture in ideology, the greater the continuity in structure.

· The USSR reproduced the Tsarist state.

· China reproduced the dynastic empire.

Each used Marxism as a vessel for the return of its pre-modern self.

7. Conclusion

The "red" color of communism concealed two very different spectrums. In Russia, it reflected iron, discipline, and faith in the state. In China, it reflected blood, lineage, and faith in moral harmony.

Communism did not erase civilization; it revealed it. The Soviet and Chinese experiments show that ideology, when transplanted, grows in the soil of culture it finds—and that the roots of power run deeper than any imported creed.

References

Fairbank, J. K. (1998). *China: A new history.* Harvard University Press.

Kotkin, S. (2014). *Stalin: Paradoxes of power, 1878–1928.* Penguin.

MacFarquhar, R. (1974). *The origins of the Cultural Revolution.* Columbia University Press.

Riasanovsky, N. V. (1992). *A history of Russia.* Oxford University Press.

Weber, M. (1951). *The religion of China and the religion of Russia.* Free Press.

The Dynasty of Juche: North Korea and the Apotheosis of Ideological Power

J. A. Springs

Independent Author & Researcher

Writing for the World Press

Unaffiliated with Academic Institution

Author Note

This paper was written as part of the author's ongoing research into ideological morphology and civilizational adaptation. It continues the comparative framework initiated in *Two Red Empires* by examining how imported doctrines evolve into local theologies of power.

Abstract

North Korea presents the ultimate mutation of the communist experiment: a hereditary theocracy masquerading as a socialist republic. This essay argues that Kim Il-sung's regime reinterpreted Marxism through Korea's Confucian and colonial legacies, producing a dynastic cult that sacralized power rather than redistributed it. By tracing Juche ideology, the cult of personality, and the mechanisms of hereditary succession, this paper shows how communism in Korea ceased to be an economic doctrine and became a political religion designed to eternalize one family's rule.

Keywords: Juche, Confucianism, political religion, autarky, North Korea, ideological adaptation

1. Introduction

No state on Earth resembles North Korea. It calls itself a Democratic People's Republic yet functions as a divine monarchy. Its ideology claims Marxist heritage yet revolves around the worship of a single bloodline.

This paradox dissolves once we recognize that North Korean communism was never Marxism translated—it was Stalinism *re-Confucianized*. Where Marx sought to abolish the family, Kim Il-sung rebuilt the nation as one: the Great Leader as father, the people as children. Revolution became filial piety writ large.

2. The Foundations: Liberation and Opportunity

In 1945, Soviet occupation created a vacuum north of the 38th parallel. Kim Il-sung, a guerrilla of modest rank, was elevated precisely because he lacked independent power. Under Soviet tutelage he learned the mechanics of Leninist party control. But he also understood that Korean society—steeped in hierarchy and scarred by Japanese colonization—hungered for a unifying patriarch.

Where Lenin spoke of proletarian vanguards, Kim spoke of national purity and self-reliance. Communism offered tools of governance; Korean tradition supplied the emotional architecture.

3. Juche: From Ideology to Theology

By the late 1950s Kim Il-sung had purged rivals and introduced *Juche* *(⟡⟡)*, or "subjectivity / self-reliance." Officially, Juche elevated man as "master of his destiny." In reality, it elevated the Leader as the master of *all* destinies.

Juche fused three elements:

1. **Marxist vocabulary** — equality and struggle.
2. **Confucian ethics** — filial loyalty to the patriarch.
3. **Korean nationalism** — purity of blood and resistance to outsiders.

The synthesis created a political religion where ideological truth emanated from the Kim family itself. The Great Leader was infallible not by logic but by lineage.

4. The Cult as Governance

The cult of personality in North Korea is not ornamental; it is the operating system.

· Portraits, badges, and rituals create omnipresent surveillance through piety.

· The state dispenses food, education, and shelter as sacraments of loyalty.

· *The Ten Principles for the Establishment of the Monolithic Ideological System* function as a catechism demanding "unconditional obedience."

The result is a closed loop: belief ensures survival, and survival confirms belief. Political failure thus becomes moral failure—a heresy against the family-state.

5. Hereditary Succession: The Return of the Dynasty

In 1994, Kim Il-sung's death could have ended the regime. Instead, power passed seamlessly to Kim Jong-il, and later to Kim Jong-un. This succession defied every Marxist principle but satisfied every Confucian one: continuity, lineage, and filial reverence. The state declared Kim Il-sung "Eternal President," ensuring perpetual legitimacy.

North Korea thus became the first hereditary communist monarchy—a contradiction only in theory. In practice, it fulfilled the deep Korean pattern of moral kingship and familial loyalty.

6. Juche Economics: Autarky as Virtue

North Korea's chronic isolation is often explained as strategic. But ideologically it functions as moral hygiene. Foreign dependence equals impurity; self-reliance equals virtue. Even famine in the 1990s was framed as a "march of hardship," a test of filial endurance. The people were not merely starving—they were suffering for their father's vision.

Economic rationality is irrelevant. The system's currency is sacrifice, not efficiency.

7. From Marxism to Myth

Marxist Principle	North Korean Transformation
Class struggle	Struggle for purity and loyalty
Abolition of family	Family as national model
Internationalism	Racial exceptionalism
Scientific socialism	Mystical nationalism
Collective ownership	Dynastic control through the Party

Kimism replaced dialectical materialism with mythic voluntarism: the Leader's will reshapes reality. Truth is performative; whatever the Leader says becomes fact. This is not ideology—it is liturgy.

8. The Function of Fear and Faith

The regime's longevity stems from two psychological engines:

· **Fear:** absolute surveillance, gulags, and the impossibility of escape.

· **Faith:** indoctrination from birth, songs, rituals, and miraculous propaganda.

Where fear fails, faith fills the gap; where faith falters, fear enforces it. Together they form a perfect totality—a totalitarianism of the soul.

9. Conclusion

North Korea represents the apotheosis of ideological power—the moment when an imported creed dissolves entirely into the local culture that hosts it. Communism became monarchy; revolution became religion.

The world often treats North Korea as a failed state; in reality, it is a fulfilled archetype—the resurrection of dynastic divinity in modern costume. Kim Il-sung did not betray Marxism; he domesticated it, turning it into the most stable form of power known to the Korean imagination: the eternal father ruling the faithful household of the nation.

References

Armstrong, C. K. (2003). *The North Korean revolution, 1945–1950.* Cornell University Press.

Cumings, B. (2005). *Korea's place in the sun.* W. W. Norton.

Lankov, A. (2013). *The real North Korea: Life and politics in the failed Stalinist utopia.* Oxford University Press.

Myers, B. R. (2010). *The cleanest race: How North Koreans see themselves and why it matters.* Melville House.

Oh, K., & Hassig, R. C. (2000). *North Korea through the looking glass.* Brookings Institution.

Part V

Clarity and Its Costs

If earlier parts traced how form, structure, and moral intent shape creative work, this final section turns to the system that frames our exchanges about knowledge itself: academic prose. While preparing these essays for publication, I used AI as a polishing tool and watched something subtle but decisive happen. Reasoning—paragraphs that showed thought moving—was compressed into conclusion. Open questions became confident claims. "Clarity," as enforced by editorial fashion and algorithmic assist, meant brevity rather than transparency.

The experience raised a larger worry. If publication norms and automation reward summaries over demonstrations, are we quietly redefining understanding as the speed of the takeaway? When the path of thought is hidden, comprehension becomes consumption.

The paper that follows, **Are We Sacrificing Understanding for Clarity?**, asks whether the academy's pursuit of readability has slid into an economy of assertions—more efficient to cite, easier to scan, thinner to think with. It is the most self-reflexive work in this volume: not a study of craft, but of the rhetorical machinery that receives, compresses, and legitimizes craft. If argument is an invitation to reason together, this essay considers what is lost when the invitation is replaced by a headline.

Are We Sacrificing Understanding for Clarity?: The Shift from Argument to Assertion and the Disappearance of Reasoning in Modern Academic Writing

J. A. Springs

Independent Author & Researcher

Writing for the World Press

Unaffiliated with Academic Institution

Author Note

This paper originated from my own experience using artificial intelligence as an editorial tool for my academic manuscripts. While AI-assisted revision offered improvements in fluency and consistency, it also revealed an unintended pattern: entire sections of reasoning—carefully constructed demonstrations of thought—were routinely condensed into brief assertions. The result, though more polished, carried less meaning. Arguments became summaries, and discussions became conclusions. This realization led me to investigate whether the same compression occurring algorithmically also mirrors broader institutional and cultural trends within academia. The following study explores that phenomenon.

Abstract

This paper examines the growing academic preference for concise assertion over extended reasoning. The modern ideal of "clarity"—once synonymous with logical transparency—has shifted toward linguistic brevity and editorial uniformity. While these conventions improve readability and publishing efficiency, they narrow the space for intellectual exposition, reducing argument to declaration. Drawing upon Aristotle's conception of discourse as collaborative reasoning, Stephen Toulmin's model of argumentation, and contemporary critiques of academic style, this study situates the transformation within the institutional and cognitive economies of modern scholarship. It argues that the decline of visible reasoning is not an intellectual failure but a systemic adaptation to constraints that prioritize production over understanding. The discussion concludes by suggesting frameworks for bridging clarity and reasoning, ensuring that academic communication remains both accessible and epistemically rigorous.

Keywords: academic writing, clarity, reasoning, rhetoric, argumentation, Aristotle, Toulmin, discourse, publication culture

1. Introduction — From Illumination to Efficiency

Modern academic writing aspires to precision but often achieves sterility. Where earlier scholarship invited readers into the motion of thought, contemporary prose presents results with minimal trace of how they were reached. The "clarity" valued today is not illumination but compression—a form of linguistic efficiency shaped by editorial and institutional pressures (Sword, 2012).

This paper does not argue for a nostalgic return to verbosity but asks what is lost when the pathway of reasoning is replaced by the static presentation of conclusions. When clarity becomes synonymous with brevity, understanding becomes secondary to immediacy.

2. The Aristotelian Foundation — Argument as Invitation

Aristotle viewed rhetoric not as manipulation but as *logos in motion*—the capacity to reason together through discourse (*Rhetoric*, trans. Kennedy, 2007). In *Posterior Analytics* (trans. Barnes, 1994), he describes demonstration (*apodeixis*) as a process by which understanding arises from causes made visible through logical progression. Argument, in this sense, is an invitation to participate in reasoning rather than an act of persuasion or display.

The academic paper inherits this lineage. It is not merely a repository of conclusions but a record of intellectual movement. When reasoning is compressed out of visibility, the dialogic function of scholarship collapses. The text ceases to invite thought and instead asserts authority—a transformation from *logos* to *statement*.

3. The Rise of Assertion — Institutional and Structural Pressures

The drift from argumentation to assertion has structural origins rather than philosophical ones. Several interlocking forces have redefined what counts as "good" academic writing:

· **Publication economics.** The mass expansion of scholarly journals and the economics of space have compressed the format of argument itself. Long-form exposition once common in monographs has been replaced by condensed "findings-oriented" papers (Montgomery, 2017).

· **Metric-driven evaluation.** The citation economy rewards easily quotable claims and penalizes exploratory reasoning. As Latour (1987) noted, modern science's authority rests on circulation, not comprehension.

· **Standardization of tone.** The dominance of style guides such as APA and the rise of journalistic conventions in scientific writing have discouraged narrative reasoning and reflective argumentation.

· **Digital consumption.** With most papers read online, brevity has become a survival mechanism in the attention economy (Carr, 2010).

These pressures collectively foster what Toulmin (1958) would call an "assertive model" of argumentation: a structure focused on claims and warrants but stripped of the reasoning that connects them. The result is rhetorical efficiency without epistemic transparency.

4. The Cognitive Cost — Understanding Without Motion

Reasoning is not a decorative flourish but a cognitive bridge. As Bruner (1986) observed, narrative and argument share a common epistemic function: both allow humans to "make the obscure plausible." When this connective tissue disappears, knowledge devolves into information—and information cannot teach.

Donald Schön (1983) referred to reflective writing as *"reflection-in-action"*—the visible trace of thought adapting to circumstance. Academic prose that erases its reasoning severs this reflection from its readers. Understanding becomes *consumed* rather than *constructed*.

Furthermore, pedagogical consequences follow. Emerging scholars, exposed only to conclusion-driven papers, internalize a style that prizes statement over process. They imitate the artifact, not the reasoning that should have animated it. The academy thus risks producing writers fluent in *presentation* but impoverished in *inference*.

5. Bridging the Divide — Clarity as Transparent Reasoning

True clarity is not synonymous with brevity. It resides in transparency—language that reveals the architecture of thought without overwhelming the reader. The challenge is to restore reasoning to visibility without forfeiting accessibility.

Several strategies may serve as bridges:

· **Layered exposition.** Following the "inverted pyramid" used in journalism, conclusions may lead, but reasoning must follow—allowing both summary and depth for different readers.

· **Reflective scaffolding.** Transitional phrasing ("from this follows," "hence it may be inferred") signals inferential motion without lengthening text unduly.

· **Dual-mode presentation.** Supplementary material, digital appendices, or interactive figures can preserve fuller argumentation outside strict word limits.

· **Editorial reframing.** Journals might evaluate clarity not by economy of language but by *fidelity of understanding achieved.*

These practices reaffirm what Toulmin (1958) called the "warrant"—the connective logic between claim and evidence—as the locus of intellectual honesty.

6. The Future of Academic Discourse — Knowledge as Process

The compression of academic reasoning mirrors a cultural shift from *knowledge as inquiry* to *knowledge as product.* In a system where intellectual labor is quantified through metrics, the value of thought lies in its visibility as output, not its capacity for exploration.

Yet, as Aristotle reminds us, reasoning is an ethical act: to persuade through logic rather than authority is to respect the autonomy of the audience. When scholars present only assertions, they exchange reasoned dialogue for rhetorical compliance. What is lost is not knowledge itself but the *experience of knowing.*

The future of academic discourse depends on remembering that understanding is not instantaneous. Comprehension arises through motion—the slow unfolding of premise into insight. If argument is the language of reason, then brevity without reasoning risks becoming the silence of thought.

7. Conclusion — The Ethics of Comprehension

The trajectory of academic writing reveals a paradox: in seeking clarity, it has often abandoned the very mechanisms by which clarity is achieved. Reasoning has become the hidden casualty of efficiency.

This paper has not argued for a regression to verbosity but for recognition of what is being traded away in the pursuit of polish. The bridge forward lies in acknowledging that clarity is not the *absence* of complexity but the *intelligibility* of it.

Aristotle's insight remains our best compass: rhetoric's highest purpose is not to win agreement but to **invite reason.** When academic prose conceals its reasoning, it closes the invitation—and with it, the door to genuine understanding.

References

Aristotle. (1994). *Posterior Analytics* (J. Barnes, Trans.). Clarendon Press.

Aristotle. (2007). *On Rhetoric: A Theory of Civic Discourse* (G. A. Kennedy, Trans.). Oxford University Press.

Bruner, J. (1986). *Actual Minds, Possible Worlds.* Harvard University Press.

Carr, N. (2010). *The Shallows: What the Internet Is Doing to Our Brains.* W. W. Norton & Company.

Latour, B. (1987). *Science in Action: How to Follow Scientists and Engineers through Society.* Harvard University Press.

Montgomery, S. L. (2017). *The Chicago Guide to Communicating Science.* University of Chicago Press.

Schön, D. A. (1983). *The Reflective Practitioner: How Professionals Think in Action.* Basic Books.

Sword, H. (2012). *Stylish Academic Writing.* Harvard University Press.

Toulmin, S. (1958). *The Uses of Argument.* Cambridge University Press.

Part VI

On Independent Mastery

This section joins two works that share no origin but trace the same pattern: mastery arising without formal inheritance.

The first, **The Form Reveals the Function**, began from frustration. While researching Prior Learning Assessment programs, I wondered if it were possible to receive academic credit for a body of writing skill built outside formal study. The answer, as it turned out, was no—at least not without translating lived fluency into institutional language. That experience became a study of how intuitive expertise resists codification, and how systems measure legitimacy by vocabulary rather than demonstration.

The second essay, **Contradiction Made Flesh**, began from curiosity rather than critique. While reading about military philosophy, I noticed how often the figure of the soldier-scholar appeared across unconnected civilizations: the philosopher-king, the Stoic general, the samurai monk. I wanted to know why. The research revealed no shared origin, only recurrence—suggesting that whenever humanity develops the power to destroy, it simultaneously invents reflection to restrain it.

Though conceived apart, both essays examine **self-taught systems**: individuals or societies discovering coherence without permission, reason emerging where structure lags behind. One concerns the individual intellect; the other, the collective conscience. Together, they explore the strange autonomy of understanding—how knowledge, whether personal or cultural, keeps finding ways to teach itself.

The Form Reveals the Function: On Internalized Mastery, Intuitive Writing, and the Gatekeeping of Academic Legitimacy

J. A. Springs

Independent Author & Researcher

Writing for the World Press

Unaffiliated with Academic Institution

Abstract

This article examines the tension between demonstrated expertise and institutional recognition in the context of intuitive writing practice. Focusing on the limitations of Prior Learning Assessment (PLA), it interrogates how internalized, experience-driven knowledge resists codification within traditional academic frameworks. Drawing on theories of tacit knowledge, implicit learning, and creative cognition, the paper reviews key models that account for expertise which eludes formal instruction or conscious articulation. Special attention is given to cognitive fluency, narrative intuition, and the affective dimensions of reader engagement. By synthesizing insights across educational psychology, literary theory, and epistemology, the paper questions prevailing assumptions about how academic legitimacy is earned, measured, and granted in the absence of credentials.

Keywords: academic recognition, creative cognition, internalized mastery, intuitive writing, meta-criticism, narrative technique, performed argument, prior learning assessment, tacit knowledge, writing pedagogy

1. Introduction

There exists a longstanding dissonance between demonstrated mastery and institutional recognition within higher education, particularly in disciplines that rely on creative and expressive output. While frameworks such as Prior Learning Assessment (PLA) and competency-based models have broadened the definition of academic legitimacy, they often fall short when confronted with forms of expertise that resist easy codification. Nowhere is this more evident than in the domain of writing—where intuition, pattern recognition, and aesthetic fluency often shape high-level output long before formal terminology is acquired. This poses a challenge to institutions: how do you assess what cannot be fully described, only observed in effect?

This paper interrogates how intuitive proficiency, particularly in written expression, remains undervalued in academic systems that privilege procedural explanation over performance. By reviewing key literature across educational theory, cognitive science, and epistemology, it questions whether existing frameworks are equipped to assess what can be demonstrated, but not always named.

The purpose of this paper is to explore that very paradox. It will examine the disjunct between the intuitive practitioner's outputs and academia's existing models for recognition. More subtly, it will do so while enacting the very methods it defends.

2. Defining Intuitive Mastery

To define intuitive mastery is to circle a flame without naming the heat. It can be traced through its outcomes, but rarely dissected without losing its essence. Ericsson & Pool (2016) discuss *"deliberate practice"* as a means toward expertise, yet this presumes that every stage is trackable, externalized, and replicable. Polanyi (1966) counters with the notion of tacit knowledge: we know more than we can tell. Intuitive mastery belongs to this domain.

The intuitive writer draws from thousands of narrative encounters, subconscious pattern recognition, emotional sequencing, and structural rhythm—none of which may be easily articulated as academic knowledge but are evidenced through execution. Cleeremans et al. (1998) reinforce this point, showing how complex learning can occur through implicit exposure, even in the absence of conscious rule formation.

Dreyfus & Dreyfus's (1980) five-stage model of skill acquisition notes that experts often *"just know"* what the next step is. Kahneman (2011) would categorize this as System 1 thinking—fast, automatic, and experience-driven. This is not anti-intellectualism; it is post-procedural literacy.

This kind of mastery does not require a formal study of proto-Indo-European root systems or the etymological lineage of conjunctions. It is instead a present-tense literacy—a lived fluency in how language is used now, by real people, in real conversations. It is the ability to discern when a word, while technically correct, rings false. To know when something 'feels written.' A practitioner of this caliber can read a set of song lyrics and know, instantly, whether they were generated by an algorithm—not by spotting a keyword, but through pattern recognition. They sense narrative dissonance, emotional incongruity, or artificial rhythm the way a seasoned musician hears a flat note.

This is not mysticism. Not luck. It is recognition. Chess grandmasters exhibit this with board positions; intuitive writers exhibit it with tone, phrasing, and flow. In both cases, the internalization is so complete that naming the technique becomes secondary to executing it flawlessly. This is not ignorance—it is beyond articulation. A performance of what has already been absorbed. As Springs (2025) argues, intuitive writing reflects a "predictive engine of exposure-hardened memory"—a rhythm learned by feel, not instruction.

3. Institutional Hostility Toward the Uncodified

Within U.S. higher education, PLA frameworks (e.g., CAEL, 2019) and **ACE** credit recommendations aim to translate experiential learning into academic credit, but they still privilege evidence that is narratable in institutional discourse.

Despite institutional gestures toward inclusivity through Prior Learning Assessment (PLA) programs, most universities still reward only what can be articulated in standardized terms. The Council for Adult and Experiential Learning (CAEL) promotes frameworks for evaluating prior knowledge, but these typically require the translation of lived, intuitive practice into academic prose. What, then, of the practitioner who writes at a publishable level across fiction, nonfiction, and academic genres—yet cannot—or chooses not to—codify their process in discipline-sanctioned language? What of the writer who could distinguish a gerund from a participle, but prefers instead to revise a paragraph until it breathes, sings, and stings exactly as intended?

Within many writing programs, legitimacy is tethered to workshops, critique sessions, and fluency in craft terminology. These are useful instruments, but not definitive indicators of mastery. And yet, academia continues to privilege the explainable over the effective, the visible process over the invisible result. The intuitive writer thus occupies a paradoxical position: producing demonstrably excellent work while being asked to justify it through terms antithetical to how it was created.

What is lost in this demand? Not only the practitioner—but the progress. The future does not always arrive wearing a syllabus. Sometimes, it begins as a paragraph no one knew how to file.

4. Literature Review: On Knowing Without Saying

The literature surrounding intuitive cognition, while extensive in psychological and philosophical domains, remains under-leveraged in academic discussions of writing pedagogy and assessment. Nevertheless, key frameworks from these adjacent fields provide a foundation for understanding how complex creative behaviors—such as writing—can emerge from deeply internalized processes rather than explicit instruction.

Research on implicit learning shows that individuals can acquire complex, rule-governed behavior without conscious awareness (Reber, 1993; Cleeremans et al., 1998). These findings are central to understanding how writers, through prolonged exposure and engagement, internalize narrative structures that guide decision-making during composition—without needing to name or explain the rules they follow.

This intuitive process aligns with dual process theory, which differentiates between System 1 (fast, automatic) and System 2 (slow, deliberate) thinking (Kahneman, 2011). Skilled writers often operate from System 1 fluency, drawing on deep reservoirs of exposure and experience, allowing instinctual narrative decisions that feel inevitable rather than calculated. They don't merely write quickly—they write from what seems to emerge all at once, fully formed, even if revised later.

The concept of flow, introduced by Csikszentmihalyi (1990), describes a state of immersive creativity in which action and awareness merge. Writers in flow bypass linear, conscious processing and instead enact pre-consolidated schemas. Polanyi's (1966) theory of tacit knowledge complements this, asserting that we can know more than we can tell. Together, these suggest that the knowledge behind high-level writing is often embodied, not articulated.

Even frameworks traditionally applied to media studies—such as Hall's (1980) encoding/decoding model—resonate here. Intuitive writers often embed multivalent cues into text, anticipating the decoding strategies of diverse readers, much as effective communicators tailor their message for multiple interpretive frames. This encoding, however, is rarely conscious in procedural terms. It feels more like tonal calibration than outline-based intent.

A particularly relevant lens comes from narrative transportation theory (Green & Brock, 2000), which shifts the focus to the reader, arguing that coherence and affective immersion matter more than structural formula. Writers who intuitively calibrate their work to feel right—in tone, pacing, and emotional arc—are often working not from genre conventions but from a deeply internalized model of emotional movement.

This pattern extends beyond fiction. In interdisciplinary research, intuitive narrative fluency shows itself through vertical modulation—the ability to shift seamlessly between conceptual abstraction and technical specificity. One such demonstration appears in Blake & Springs (2025), which critiques AI self-preservation assumptions. There, intuitive cognition operates not through metaphor, but structure: transitioning from ontology to operational logic to ethical implications with a fluidity rarely taught, but often recognized. The paper didn't tell a story. But it thought like one.

These frameworks converge on a shared recognition: that intuitive behavior is measurable in output, even when it evades internal explanation. What's missing, however, is a pedagogical model—or an institutional framework—that trusts the work when the words to describe the process won't come. Until such a model exists, mastery without method remains suspect. And writers who know without saying will remain, at best, misunderstood.

5. The Performed Argument

What would it mean to structure an academic paper not just as a linear argument, but as a performance? Not performance in the theatrical sense, but in the sense of enacting the very claim one seeks to make—letting form embody content.

In traditional academic writing, structure is often segmented: literature, theory, method, conclusion. Transitions are linear, tone consistent, the voice disembodied. But what if an argument about intuitive mastery in writing were itself constructed intuitively—shaped by rhythm, affect, and recursive logic, rather than fixed templates? What if the paper unfolded more like a novel or essay, using rising tension, tonal shifts, and thematic layering to draw the reader into the argument, rather than simply laying it out?

Such a structure would need to obscure its intent until later—delaying the revelation of design in favor of experiential immersion. Early sections might maintain the expected academic tone and citation style. But behind them would be narrative scaffolding: rhythmically linked paragraphs, recursive phrasing, and internal echoes that don't merely state an idea, but stage it.

It would rely on transitions that feel natural rather than sound mechanical, and a momentum not of segmented analysis but of rising tension—eventually cresting in a meta-critical turn. The reader might not immediately notice this choreography. But they'd feel it. And upon rereading, they might realize that what appeared to be conventional structure was, in fact, something else entirely.

This approach would not be decorative. It would be a functional argument. Because if intuitive mastery is real—if it can shape prose without formula—then shouldn't a paper defending that idea show as much as it tells?

The conditions required for this kind of writing are rare: deep familiarity with genre, academic credibility sufficient to risk deviation, and an audience open to layered argument. But when successful, such a paper would not just describe intuition.

It would become evidence of it.

6. On Structure and Intent: A Meta-Critical Reflection

This is the moment we step outside the frame.

Everything described in the previous section—recursive rhythm, tonal modulation, thematic scaffolding, withheld context—has already happened. This paper did not merely propose a 'performed' argument. It was one.

What you've read was structured to be experienced before it was explained. The academic tone was deliberate. So was the shift. The pacing, the transitions, the gradual thematic layering—none of it followed a conventional thesis model, though it wore the costume. Instead, the paper moved like an essay, thought like a short story, and delayed its reveal like a novel. It was intuitive, but not improvised. It was structured, but not formulaic.

This wasn't sleight of hand. It was craft. The kind you can't always name but recognize in motion. Kolb (1984) and Eraut (2000) informed that many individuals know more than they can tell. They are then reduced to 'showing' instead. What looked like literature review was rising action; what sounded like method was staging.

Where a traditional literature review segmented findings, this one bled. Where an institutional critique might rely on policy analysis, this one pulsed with rhetorical pressure. Where a methodological section might cite precedent, this one became its own test case. Narrative techniques were embedded not to entertain, but to prove the central thesis: *that intuitive writing is a legitimate mode of mastery—even, and especially, when it eludes codification.*

The late structural turn—the one happening now—mirrors what fiction calls a reveal: the moment you realize the frame was never what you thought. Every earlier section reads differently now. That's the point.

Barthes told us the author is dead. But the architect is not. bell hooks taught us that presence is pedagogy. This paper's presence was always performative. Graff and Birkenstein reminded us that academic moves can be taught like choreography—but choreography, once mastered, becomes dance.

And this paper danced.

7. Conclusion and Call to Action

This paper set out to explore a paradox: the tension between intuitive writing and institutional recognition. It examined the disjunct between the outputs of practiced, genre-fluid writers and academia's rigid, credentialed models for validation. But more than that—it performed the very methods it defends.

It argued that intuitive mastery is real.

Demonstrable. Transferable. And too often, overlooked.

Once internalized, such mastery transcends genre, discipline, and mode. It becomes a portable architecture—responsive, adaptive, precise (Perkins & Salomon, 1992). Yet the academy still favors credentials over competence, procedure over proof, legibility over lived skill. In doing so, it risks missing what matters most: *the work itself.*

If that sounds abstract, revisit the form of this essay. Read again. Trace the progression. Feel the rhythm. Watch the reveal unfold. Every pivot, every echo, every tonal modulation—it was designed, not declared. This wasn't just an argument.

It was evidence.

Formally, this essay performs its thesis: its structure enacts intuitive mastery while wearing academic dress. It was easier for me to show what I knew than to tell what I knew (Polanyi, 1966).

Still skeptical?

Then I offer this:

"If you think I'm bluffing, ask me to write another journal article like this.

Or... wait a month. Check my catalogue.

Wait another month. Check again.

My back catalogue speaks for itself."

Legitimacy, here, is evidenced by durable output rather than credentialed narration of process.

As writers, we're encouraged to 'show, don't tell.'

I just made it literal.

8. Author's Note on Writing Assistance

Portions of this manuscript were revised with the assistance of an AI-based language model to improve clarity, structure, and formatting. All ideas, arguments, interpretations, and original text were developed by the author. The AI was used solely as a post-draft polishing tool under human supervision.

References

American Council on Education (ACE). (n.d.). *ACE Credit®*.

Barthes, R. (1977). *Image, music, text* (S. Heath, Trans.). Hill and Wang.

Blake, K., & Springs, J. A. (2025). *The limits of instrumental reasoning in artificial agents: A critique of assumed self-preservation without self-awareness.*

CAEL. (2019). *Fueling the Race to Postsecondary Success: A 48-Institution Study of Prior Learning Assessment and Adult Student Outcomes* (updated ed.).

Cleeremans, A., Destrebecqz, A., & Boyer, M. (1998). Implicit learning: News from the front. *Trends in Cognitive Sciences, 2*(10), 406–416. https://doi.org/10.1016/S1364-6613(98)01232-7

Csikszentmihalyi, M. (1990). *Flow: The psychology of optimal experience.* Harper & Row.

Dreyfus, H. L., & Dreyfus, S. E. (1980). *A five-stage model of the mental activities involved in directed skill acquisition* (Report No. ORC-80-2). University of California, Berkeley, Operations Research Center.

Eraut, M. (2000). *Non-formal learning and tacit knowledge in professional work. British Journal of Educational Psychology, 70*(1), 113-136.

Ericsson, A., & Pool, R. (2016). *Peak: Secrets from the new science of expertise.* Houghton Mifflin Harcourt.

Graff, G., & Birkenstein, C. (2016). *They say / I say: The moves that matter in academic writing* (3rd ed.). W. W. Norton & Company.

Green, M. C., & Brock, T. C. (2000). The role of transportation in the persuasiveness of public narratives. *Journal of Personality and Social Psychology,* 79(5), 701–721. https://doi.org/10.1037/0022-3514.79.5.701

Hall, S. (1980). Encoding/decoding. In S. Hall, D. Hobson, A. Lowe, & P. Willis (Eds.), *Culture, media, language* (pp. 128–138). Hutchinson.

hooks, b. (1994). *Teaching to transgress: Education as the practice of freedom.* Routledge.

Kahneman, D. (2011). *Thinking, fast and slow.* Farrar, Straus and Giroux.

Kolb, D. A. (1984). *Experiential learning.*

Perkins, D. N., Salomon, G. (1992). *Transfer of learning. International Encyclopedia of Education.*

Polanyi, M. (1966). *The tacit dimension.* University of Chicago Press.

Reber, A. S. (1993). *Implicit learning and tacit knowledge: An essay on the cognitive unconscious.* Oxford University Press.

Springs, J. A. (2025). *Narrative intuition as predictive momentum: A computational metaphor for intuitive writing practice.* Writing for the World Press (forthcoming).

Contradiction Made Flesh - The Pen and the Sword in Disparate Civilizations: An Exploration of the Independent Emergence of the Soldier-Philosopher Ideal

J. A. Springs

Independent Author & Researcher

Writing for the World Press

Unaffiliated with Academic Institution

Abstract

Across civilizations, a recurring figure stands at the threshold between power and reflection: the warrior who contemplates, the monk who fights, the ruler who writes. From Plato's *philosopher-king* in *The Republic* (Plato, trans. Bloom, 1968) to the Roman emperor Marcus Aurelius composing *Meditations* in a war camp (Aurelius, trans. Hays, 2002), from the Japanese samurai's *bunbu ryōdō*—"the dual way of the brush and the sword" (Waley, 1957)—to the martial monks of Shaolin (Shahar, 2008), cultures separated by vast distances and divergent languages each produced the same paradox: mastery of destruction joined to mastery of understanding. This essay does not claim to know *why* this convergence occurred but explores *how* and *why it might have been inevitable*, a product of shared human pressures rather than historical exchange.

I. The Recurrence of a Paradox

Each society that celebrated the sword eventually discovered the need for its counterweight. In Greece, *sophrosyne*—temperance and self-command—was considered as essential to the guardian as courage (Plato, *Republic*). Rome joined *virtus* to *sapientia*, valor to wisdom (Seneca, trans. Campbell, 1969). In Japan, *Bushidō* fused martial rigor with Zen introspection, while in China the Shaolin monks merged spiritual and physical discipline in defense of their monasteries.

These examples are not simple coincidences. They suggest an emergent human pattern: wherever the act of violence becomes institutionalized, reflection follows as its ethical twin. The philosopher-warrior arises not as a curiosity but as a mechanism of equilibrium—an embodied argument that force must justify itself through thought.

II. Structural Convergence Without Cultural Contact

The persistence of this archetype across unconnected civilizations invites consideration of what Meir Shahar (2008) calls "parallel invention" in religious and martial development. Greece and Japan, Rome and Shaolin, shared no common theological or linguistic root, yet produced the same synthesis.

Such convergence likely stems from analogous structural pressures:

1. **The need to moralize power.** Aristotle's *Nicomachean Ethics* argues that virtue lies in the mean between extremes (Aristotle, trans. Ross, 1908); societies that live by war must therefore teach restraint.
2. **The psychology of reconciliation.** A warrior must integrate the trauma of violence; reflection becomes a survival tool as much as an ethical one.
3. **The pedagogy of discipline.** Martial and contemplative training rely on the same neural circuits of repetition, rhythm, and attentional control—what cognitive science now

associates with flow states.

From this perspective, the philosopher-warrior is not imported myth but a natural response to identical cognitive and social conditions: when destruction becomes necessary, introspection becomes adaptive.

III. The Pen as the Sword's Mirror

Plato's guardians studied both gymnastics and music, believing that strength untempered by grace produced brutality (Plato, *Republic*). Marcus Aurelius wrote that "the mind of the man in arms must also be the mind at peace with itself" (*Meditations*, 6.30). The samurai, guided by Zen, pursued *mushin*—the "no-mind" state that dissolves ego in the moment of action (Waley, 1957).

Though separated by continents, each tradition taught the same equilibrium: mastery outward requires mastery inward. The pen and sword, then, are not opposites but mirrors—each reflecting discipline, rhythm, and moral intent.

IV. Cognitive Parallels and Anthropological Plausibility

Anthropological studies of ritual and performance suggest that repetitive physical training—whether in calligraphy, prayer, or combat—produces similar neurocognitive outcomes: heightened attention, suppressed self-referential thought, and a sense of transcendence. Such states, long described in religious terms, may explain why monks and soldiers both speak of calm amid chaos.

If these cognitive effects are universal, the emergence of reflective warriors becomes a matter not of diffusion but of *neurological convergence*. The Shaolin monk, the Stoic general, and the samurai poet all engage the same circuitry of presence and control.

V. The Social Necessity of the Contradiction

Beyond the personal, societies appear to require this figure to stabilize themselves. A culture that venerates only warriors risks tyranny; one that venerates only scholars risks fragility. The soldier-philosopher, in any form, embodies equilibrium—a recognition that survival and morality must coexist. As Seneca observed, "To be brave is not to rage, but to endure with reason."

It is perhaps inevitable, then, that civilizations rediscover this living contradiction whenever they reach a threshold between chaos and order.

VI. Conclusion: The Enduring Mirror

The repeated rise of the soldier-philosopher suggests that human beings, regardless of culture, intuit the need to reconcile power with wisdom. Whether expressed through the Stoic emperor, the contemplative samurai, or the monk who fights for peace, the archetype persists because it resolves the most fundamental human paradox: that we are creatures capable of both violence and reflection.

The pen and the sword, far from opposites, remain the twin instruments through which civilizations attempt to understand and restrain themselves.

References

Aristotle. (1908). *Nicomachean Ethics* (W. D. Ross, Trans.). Oxford: Clarendon Press.

Aurelius, M. (2002). *Meditations* (G. Hays, Trans.). New York: Modern Library.

Musashi, M. (2002). *The Book of Five Rings* (W. S. Wilson, Trans.). Tokyo: Kodansha.

Plato. (1968). *The Republic* (A. Bloom, Trans.). New York: Basic Books.

Seneca. (1969). *Letters from a Stoic* (R. Campbell, Trans.). London: Penguin Classics.

Shahar, M. (2008). *The Shaolin Monastery: History, Religion, and the Chinese Martial Arts.* Honolulu: University of Hawai'i Press.

Waley, A. (1957). *Zen Buddhism and the Samurai Tradition.* London: George Allen & Unwin.

Part VII

On the Temptation to Explain Everything

I live with two cats.

They are affectionate in ways that rarely align with my convenience. When I write, they walk across the keyboard. When I compose music, they brush against the faders. When I read, they sit precisely on the page I'm looking at—never another.

And yet, when I move to another room, they follow me there, find a corner, and fall asleep. No affection demanded. No gesture reciprocated. Just presence.

For a long time, I mistook this for contradiction.

I wondered, as many cat owners do, why they seemed to alternate between intimacy and indifference, why their attention came only when I was most focused elsewhere. But in one of those absurdly self-aware moments that writers have too often, I realized the question said more about *me* than them.

I had begun theorizing my cats.

I had applied the same habits I bring to writing, to thought, to scholarship—pattern recognition, cause and effect, meaning-making—to a pair of animals who were simply existing. I was studying them like a system. I was, quite literally, over-intellectualizing affection.

That's when the joke emerged.

It began as a note to myself, a way to step back from the reflex to analyze everything to death.

Why Are Cats Assholes? was never about cats. It was about projection—the way we impose coherence on the world and call it understanding. It was about how easily the desire to know becomes the need to explain, until even silence starts to demand a theory.

This short piece that follows—equal parts parody and sincerity—is my way of conceding that impulse. It's the scholar's version of laughing at himself.

Because the truth is, my cats aren't assholes.

They're just cats.

And sometimes, the simplest explanation deserves to be the final word.

Why Are Cats Assholes?: A Query into Understanding Feline Behavior

J. A. Springs

Independent Author & Researcher

Writing for the World Press

Unaffiliated with Academic Institution

Abstract

Feline behavior has long been a source of human frustration and fascination. Cat owners frequently describe their companions as aloof, unpredictable, or even antagonistic. This inquiry argues that what is interpreted as "asshole" behavior in cats reflects human discomfort with autonomy and indifference rather than evidence of feline spite.

1. Introduction: The Perception of Malice

Humans, when confronted with behavior that resists interpretation, invent narratives to reconcile dissonance. Cats disregard commands, reject affection, and maintain an unnerving sense of independence. To human observers conditioned toward reciprocity, such indifference feels personal. The term "asshole," therefore, functions as an ethological descriptor—a linguistic defense against perceived rejection.

2. Anthropomorphism and Projection

Research in comparative cognition suggests that humans consistently over-ascribe agency and intention to non-human animals (Epley, Waytz, & Cacioppo, 2007; de Waal, 2016). The cat's disinterest, when viewed through this lens, becomes a mirror for human expectation. We interpret feline autonomy through social frameworks meant for cooperative species. When cats fail to conform to those expectations, we infer defiance. Yet, as Dennett (1987) notes in his theory of the intentional stance, the appearance of intention need not correspond to any internal state. The so-called "asshole cat" is, in reality, an indifferent observer.

But why do humans insist on doing this? Because they can.

3. Conclusion

Cats are not assholes. They are participants in a separate ontology—one that resists moral mapping. Their behavior becomes "assholery" only when refracted through human expectation. The problem, therefore, is not feline temperament but with owners of cats. Cats aren't assholes, so stop projecting.

Keywords: feline behavior, anthropomorphism, projection, intentional stance, human–animal perception

Author's Note:

This paper was written during a period of prolonged feline observation and mild existential reflection. Any resemblance between the described behavior and the author's own is purely correlative.

References

Dennett, D. C. (1987). *The intentional stance.* MIT Press.

Epley, N., Waytz, A., & Cacioppo, J. T. (2007). On seeing human: A three-factor theory of anthropomorphism. *Psychological Review, 114*(4), 864–886. https://doi.org/10.1037/0033-295X.114.4.864

de Waal, F. (2016). *Are we smart enough to know how smart animals are?* W. W. Norton & Company.

Postscript: On the Origin of This Inquiry

The idea for this essay came about entirely by accident. I was editing this very book when I left my office to get Tylenol from the upstairs bathroom. One of my cats—who had been sleeping quietly nearby—followed me up the stairs, laid down and waited in the doorway while I got the medicine, and then followed me back down to the office, returning to the same chair to sleep again. The whole errand lasted less than a minute.

For reasons I can't entirely justify, I found the gesture both endearing and slightly irritating. I remember thinking, *I didn't need an escort to take a pill.* And then, almost instantly, I began analyzing the behavior—constructing theories about affection, attachment, and the absurdity of supervision from a creature that ignored me half the day until I got ready to do something I needed to focus on.

That moment was when I realized I was doing it again—applying systems thinking to a cat. The essay that followed was written as a reminder to myself to let some things simply exist without needing to be explained. It's both a parody of analysis and a confession of the inability to stop analyzing.

Included here without revision. It seemed fitting that the final word on systems and being would come from a cat. No cats were harmed in the creation of this essay.

Addendum:

They still do it, by the way. Every time. Philosophically infuriating—I still think my cats can be assholes at times. Why do you wait until right after I perfectly clean your litter box to take a shit. As if you'd been holding it in all day just so I could give you fresh litter in which to lay a turd.

Afterword

by J. A. Springs

This collection exists because I finally stopped waiting for permission to publish what I had already learned.

For years, I wrote these papers between other responsibilities—teaching, editing for others, serving in the military, and living the kind of life that teaches in ways classrooms never can. Each essay was an act of reflection, not ambition. I wasn't trying to prove anything, only to clarify what I'd come to understand about craft, ethics, and expression. The habits that built this book were formed long before I ever thought to call them scholarship. I wrote papers in college, I graded them as an adjunct professor at the Pennsylvania College of Art and Design, and I edited them for my fellow soldiers who just wanted to pass a course or finish a degree. Somewhere in all that, the habit of inquiry never left me.

Publishing through traditional channels proved more difficult than I anticipated. The gatekeepers of academic discourse tend to favor credentials, not contribution. The irony, of course, is that the very ideas explored in these essays—the legitimacy of intuitive mastery, the ethics of independence, the value of uncredentialed expertise—are what made them unwelcome in many of those same spaces. So I decided to collect them here, not as rebellion but as demonstration: that independent thought can stand on its own merit, that one's body of work can be its own credential.

This book is, in that sense, not a résumé but a record. It documents a lifelong conversation with learning itself. *Each essay captures a moment of discovery—a junction where theory and experience met and refused to separate again.* I did not write them to advance my career or to climb any ladder of recognition. I wrote them because this is how I think best: through language, through structure, through articulation. Writing remains the most honest mirror I have ever held up to my own understanding.

The language of these essays is intentionally academic. That was a conscious decision, not to mimic the conventions of scholarship but to communicate fluently with those who inhabit that world. I wanted these works to be accessible to readers who approach ideas through disciplinary lenses—philosophy, literary theory, cognitive science, or aesthetics—without requiring them to translate my intent from the outside. Writing in that shared lexicon allowed me to bridge worlds: the independent and the institutional, the intuitive and the analytical.

In publishing them together, I wanted to preserve that continuity—to show that intellectual curiosity doesn't require a syllabus, that the mind can remain in dialogue with itself long after the classroom lights have gone out.

I never really stopped going to school. I simply replaced the lecture hall with a blank page.

These essays, then, are not academic in the institutional sense, but they are academic in spirit. They belong to the long tradition of those who write to learn, who document thought not to persuade but to preserve. They stand as proof that the discipline of inquiry can survive outside the systems built to contain it.

And that, perhaps, is what I hope readers take from this collection—not the individual arguments, but the permission to keep learning without waiting to be told how.

Acknowledgments

My gratitude begins with my family—who kept insisting I was smarter than I believed and who had the patience to remind me that knowing and understanding are not the same thing. Their faith in me made it harder to hide behind modesty and forced me to recognize the depth of what I already carried within.

I also owe thanks to my friend, **Kevin Blake**, who never stopped suggesting that I go back to school and earn my doctorate. I chose not to, not out of dismissal but out of realization: that learning had already become my life, and the degree I sought was the quiet one—awarded through curiosity, persistence, and reflection. His encouragement helped me see that validation doesn't have to come from the system that trained you to seek it.

To everyone who ever asked a question that made me think harder, to every reader who met these ideas with patience and curiosity—thank you. You made the work worth refining. Thank you.

J. A. Springs is a retired veteran of the United States Army, where he served for twenty years. A father of six, he now spends his time writing, studying, and reflecting—pursuing knowledge not for recognition, but for its own sake. His work bridges philosophy, creative theory, and narrative craft, exploring how language shapes ethical understanding and emotional truth.

As the founder of *Writing for the World Press*, Springs continues to publish both fiction and nonfiction that challenge the boundaries between intuition and intellect, independence and institution. He writes not to teach, but to learn—and to leave behind a record of that ongoing education.

Collected References and Bibliographic Note

The following works have informed, influenced, or directly appeared across the essays in this volume. Some are cited explicitly; others functioned as silent companions—texts that shaped my thinking long before I learned their names. They are listed here not to display lineage, but to acknowledge continuity: that every act of writing stands on a network of thought far older than itself.

Primary Theoretical and Philosophical Works

Booth, Wayne C. *The Company We Keep: An Ethics of Fiction.* University of California Press, 1988.

Csikszentmihalyi, Mihaly. *Flow: The Psychology of Optimal Experience.* Harper & Row, 1990.

Dreyfus, Hubert L., and Stuart E. Dreyfus. *Mind over Machine: The Power of Human Intuition and Expertise in the Era of the Computer.* Free Press, 1986.

Kahneman, Daniel. *Thinking, Fast and Slow.* Farrar, Straus and Giroux, 2011.

McHale, Brian. *The Cambridge Introduction to Postmodernism.* Cambridge University Press, 2013.

Nussbaum, Martha C. *Love's Knowledge: Essays on Philosophy and Literature.* Oxford University Press, 1990.

Phelan, James. *Experiencing Fiction: Judgments, Progressions, and the Rhetorical Theory of Narrative.* Ohio State University Press, 2007.

Polanyi, Michael. *The Tacit Dimension.* Routledge & Kegan Paul, 1966.

Reber, Arthur S. "Implicit Learning of Artificial Grammars." *Journal of Verbal Learning and Verbal Behavior,* vol. 6, no. 6, 1967, pp. 855–863.

Schön, Donald A. *The Reflective Practitioner: How Professionals Think in Action.* Basic Books, 1983.

Select Works in Cognitive Science, Artificial Intelligence, and Ethics

Bostrom, Nick. "The Superintelligent Will: Motivation and Instrumental Rationality in Advanced Artificial Agents." 2012, https://nickbostrom.com/superintelligentwill.pdf.

Hadfield-Menell, Dylan, et al. "The Off-Switch Game." *arXiv preprint* arXiv:1611.08219, 2016.

Russell, Stuart J. "Elon Musk's Billion-Dollar Crusade to Stop the A.I. Apocalypse." *Vanity Fair,* 26 Mar. 2017.

Ward, F. R. "Towards a Theory of AI Personhood." *arXiv preprint* arXiv:2501.13533, 2025.

Zeng, Y., Li, J., & Zhu, Q. "Brain-Inspired and Self-Based Artificial Intelligence." *arXiv preprint* arXiv:2402.18784, 2024.

Supplementary and Referenced Creative Texts

Springs, J. A. *Boundless Fragments: A Collection of a Novella and Short Stories.* Writing for the World Press, 2025.

Springs, J. A. *The One I Let Go: An Elegy for a Sentence.* Unpublished manuscript, Writing for the World Press, 2024.

Acknowledgment of Influence

In addition to these references, this collection owes an invisible debt to the ongoing conversation between art and reason—the countless unnamed voices, living and dead, whose ideas ripple through language itself.

This collection also owes much to the open classrooms of the modern world—the conversations and demonstrations shared through platforms such as *Veritasium*, *Astrum*, and *The Military Show*, which continue the work of bringing complex ideas into public discourse.

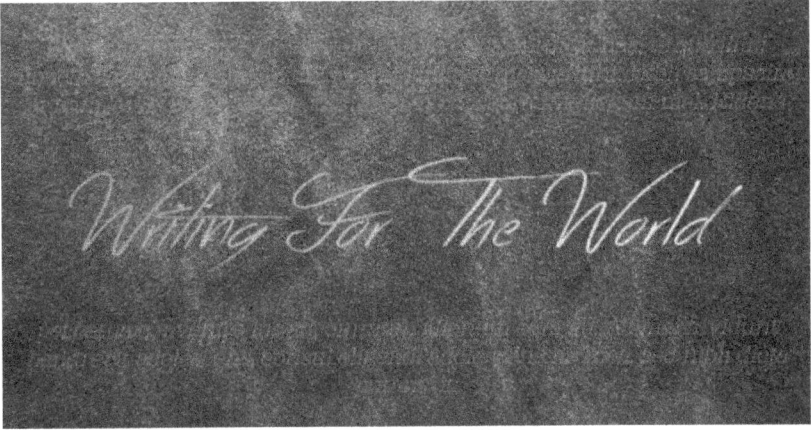

https://writingfortheworldpress.com

Also by J. A. Springs

Chronicles of Cosmic Realms
Shadows of the Forgotten Void

elctrcsheepdrmwrks (Electric Sheep Dreamworks)
Blurred Vision
Fractured
Zero One

Essays in Systems and Being
Essays in Systems and Being

The Absurdities Anthology
How Not to Find Your Local Weed-Man

The Gifted
The Untamed Force
Next Exit

The Shepherd Series
The Bad Shepherd
The Good Wolf

Standalone
Sundrops
Behind the Red Door
Boundless Fragments: A Collection of Novellas and Short Stories
Fragments of Forever

Watch for more at https://writingfortheworldpress.com.

About the Publisher

LLC. Lancaster, PA

www.writingfortheworldpress.com

Read more at https://www.writingfortheworldpress.com.

www.ingramcontent.com/pod-product-compliance
Lightning Source LLC
Chambersburg PA
CBHW071130280326
41935CB00010B/1168